America Under Attack:
September 11, 2001

Other titles in the Lucent Terrorism Library are:

America Under Attack: Primary Sources
The History of Terrorism
Terrorists and Terrorist Groups

THE
LUCENT
TERRORISM
LIBRARY

America Under Attack:
September 11, 2001

Gail B. Stewart

LUCENT BOOKS
SAN DIEGO, CALIFORNIA

THOMSON
─────✳─────™
GALE

Detroit • New York • San Diego • San Francisco
Boston • New Haven, Conn. • Waterville, Maine
London • Munich

On Cover: Flight 175 crashes into the south
tower of New York's World Trade Center.

Library of Congress Cataloging-in-Publication Data

Stewart, Gail B., 1949–
   America Under Attack: September 11, 2001 / by Gail B. Stewart.
      p.   cm. — (Terrorism library series)
Includes bibliographical references and index.
Summary: Discusses the terrorist attacks on the World Trade Center and the Pentagon on September
11, 2001, and describes their impact on the American people.
   ISBN 1-59018-208-1 (hardpack : alk. paper)
   1. September 11 Terrorist Attacks, 2001—Juvenile literature. 2. Terrorism—New York (State)—
New York—Juvenile literature. 3. Terrorism—United States—Juvenile literature. 4. Disasters—New
York (State)—New York—Juvenile literature. [1. September 11 Terrorist Attacks, 2001. 2. Terrorism.]
I. Title.   II. Series.
   HV6432 .S74 2002
   973.931—dc21

2001007506

Copyright 2002 by Lucent Books,
an imprint of The Gale Group
10911 Technology Place, San Diego, California 92127

Printed in the U.S.A.

Contents

Foreword

It was the bloodiest day in American history since the battle of Antietam during the Civil War—a day in which everything about the nation would change forever. People, when speaking of the country, would henceforth specify "before September 11" or "after September 11." It was as if, on that Tuesday morning, the borders of the United States had suddenly shifted to include Canada and Mexico, or as if the official language had changed. The difference between "before" and "after" was that pronounced.

That Tuesday morning, September 11, 2001, was the day that Americans began to learn firsthand about terrorism, as first one fuel-heavy commercial airliner, and then a second, hit New York's World Trade Towers—sending them thundering to the ground in a firestorm of smoke and ash. A third airliner was flown into a wall of the Pentagon in Washington, D.C., and a fourth was apparently wrestled away from terrorists before it could be steered into another building. By the time the explosions and collapses had stopped and the fires had been extinguished, more than three thousand Americans had died.

Film clips and photographs showed the horror of that day. Trade Center workers could be seen leaping to their deaths from seventy, eighty, ninety floors up rather than endure the 1,000-degree temperatures within the towers. New Yorkers who had thought they were going to work, were caught on film desperately racing the other way to escape the wall of dust and debris that rolled down the streets of lower Manhattan. Photographs showed badly burned Pentagon secretaries and frustrated rescue workers. Later pictures would show huge fire engines buried under the rubble.

It was not the first time America had been the target of terrorists. The same World Trade Center had been targeted in 1993 by Islamic terrorists, but the results had been negligible. The worst of such acts on American soil came in 1995 at the hands of a home-grown terrorist whose hatred for the government led to the bombing of the federal building in Oklahoma City. The blast killed 168 people—19 of them children.

But the September 11 attacks were far different. It was terror on a frighteningly well-planned, larger scale, carried out by nineteen men from the Middle East whose hatred of the United States drove them to the most appalling suicide mission the world had ever witnessed. As one U.S. intelligence officer told a CNN reporter, "These guys turned airplanes into weapons of mass destruction, landmarks familiar to all of us into mass graves."

Some observers say that September 11 may always be remembered as the date that the people of the United States finally came face to face with terrorism. "You've been relatively sheltered from terrorism," says an Israeli terrorism expert. "You hear about it happening here in the Middle East, in Northern Ireland, places far away from you. Now Americans have joined the real world where this ugliness is almost a daily occurrence."

This "real world" presents a formidable challenge to the United States and other nations. It is a world in which there are no rules, where modern terrorism is war not waged on soldiers, but on innocent people—including children. Terrorism is meant to shatter people's hope, to create instability in their daily lives, to make them feel vulnerable and frightened. People who continue to feel unsafe will demand that their leaders make concessions—*do something*—so that terrorists will stop the attacks.

Many experts feel that terrorism against the United States is just beginning. "The tragedy is that other groups, having seen [the success of the September 11 attacks] will think: why not do something else?" says Richard Murphy, former ambassador to Syria and Saudi Arabia. "This is the beginning of their war. There is a mentality at work here that the West is not prepared to understand."

Because terrorism is abhorrent to the vast majority of the nations on the planet, President George W. Bush's declaration of war against terrorism was supported by many other world leaders. He reminded citizens that it would be a long war, and one not easily won. However, as many agree, there is no choice; if terrorism is allowed to continue unchecked the world will never be safe.

The four volumes of the Lucent Terrorism Library help to explain the unexplainable events of September 11, 2001 as well as examine the history and personalities connected with terrorism in the United States and elsewhere in the world. Annotated bibliographies provide readers with ideas for further research. Fully documented primary and secondary source quotations enliven the text. Each book in this series provides students with a wealth of information as well as launching points for further study and discussion.

"The Worst of What Humanity Can Do"

The date of September 11, 2001, is one of those rare days that people will keep in their memories their whole lives. Just as they remember the date of the bombing of Pearl Harbor in World War II, or that of the assassination of President John F. Kennedy, Americans will forever recall exactly where they were when they first heard the grim news of September 11. While other events may fade from memory, Americans will never forget what they were doing when four commercial airliners were hijacked— when two destroyed the World Trade Center, one hit the Pentagon, and another crashed in Pennsylvania. It was the most horrific terrorist act in history.

"Do I Let Them Have a Few More Moments of Peace?"

Many young Americans heard the news in school, for the attacks occurred just as many students were beginning their morning classes. Their parents heard about it at work, at home, or on their car radios. Clare Arthur was on a morning run along a path near her house with her headset tuned to an FM radio station. She said the news made her stop in her tracks.

"I heard that a plane had hit the World Trade Center in New York," says Clare. "And I thought to myself, 'How horrible!' But just minutes later, the announcers broke in and said a second plane had flown into another tower. And I knew, as everyone must have known then, that we'd been attacked.

"I remember my heart just pounding, feeling weak and frightened. And I looked at other people, you know, on the path. And I remember I wanted to grab someone by the arm and say, 'Isn't that horrible, what just happened?' But no one seemed to be listening to the radio; no one knew. Everyone just kept running or walking, talking to their friends, smiling. I thought, 'Do I tell them? Or do I let them have a few more moments of peace?'" [1]

Panic and Questions

Over the next few hours, of course, the entire world learned of the tragedies in New York City, in Washington, D.C., and in western Pennsylvania. They learned that four planes were hijacked from U.S. airports, that three of them had been effectively used as missiles, each with a cargo of frightened passengers. The fourth crashed, presumably before it could hit whatever target it had been assigned.

People were horrified as they sat in front of television screens watching the scenes of explosions, fire, and death. As the twin towers of the World Trade Center collapsed, with thousands of workers still inside, the surrounding area was buried in untold millions of tons of blazing rubble. And as the nation was reeling from the news in New York, a third plane hit the Pentagon. Within minutes, a fourth plane would crash in a remote area of western Pennsylvania, almost certainly, it seemed, as a result of passengers revolting against the men who had hijacked the plane.

Throughout the nation's capital, as in New York City, panic and fear prevailed. The same frantic questions were being

Students at Brigham Young University watch a campus television stunned as news of the terrorist attacks is broadcast.

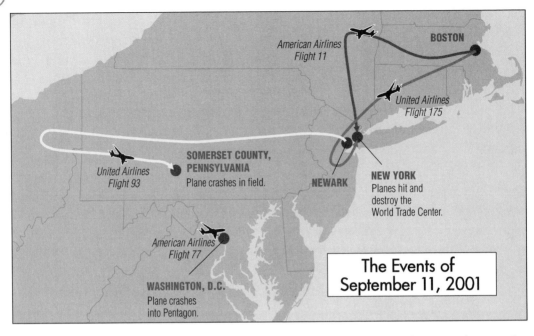

American Airlines
Flight 11

BOSTON

United Airlines
Flight 175

United Airlines
Flight 93

SOMERSET COUNTY,
PENNSYLVANIA
Plane crashes in field.

NEWARK

NEW YORK
Planes hit and
destroy the
World Trade Center.

American Airlines
Flight 77

WASHINGTON, D.C.
Plane crashes
into Pentagon.

**The Events of
September 11, 2001**

asked in both cities, and by millions watching the spectacle unfolding on television: What is happening? How many have been killed? What is next?

All Americans Were Casualties

The events of September 11, 2001, made that day the bloodiest on U.S. soil since the Civil War. But as one writer noted, unlike a true war, this horror was played out "not with soldiers, but with secretaries, security guards, lawyers, bankers, janitors."[2] It was played out, too, with passengers on civilian airplanes, and with police, firefighters, and other emergency workers.

Thousands of people were killed; however, in another sense, all Americans were casualties, too. The uneasiness, the fear, the grief, the feeling of having lost control of the future—these were the ongoing wounds

of the living. In less than two hours, the United States—the strongest nation in the world—had suffered the unimaginable. "We're going to look on this as the day everything changed," wept one New York rescue worker. "It just feels like nothing's ever going to be the same again."[3]

While massive changes would surely happen, bright spots surfaced, too—stories of astonishing bravery, compassion, and heroism during the attacks and rescue attempts. Most people would agree that September 11, 2001, will long be remembered as a tragic date in American history. It will probably also be remembered as a date that brought out a sense of unity and community in America that had not been evident before. As one woman said of her fellow New Yorkers, "We've seen the worst of what humanity can do, but now we're seeing the best."[4]

Chapter One

"The Mouth of Hell"

The morning of September 11 dawned cool and clear with the promise of a lovely fall day. On the East Coast, the sky was a shade of blue that airline pilots often call "severe clear" because of its seemingly infinite visibility. Just before 8:00 A.M., American Airlines Flight 11, a large Boeing 767, took off from Logan Airport in Boston. It was headed to Los Angeles with eighty-one passengers and crew members on board.

"He Wanted Us to Know Something Was Wrong"

The large aircraft had been traveling west for less than half an hour when suddenly it made a sharp left turn to head south, toward New York. Although no one knows exactly when, four terrorists had broken into the cockpit and seized control of the plane over Pennsylvania.

Ground controllers were aware that there was serious trouble aboard the air-craft very soon after terrorists took control. The pilot secretly depressed a special button on the airplane's steering mechanism. Called a "push-to-talk button," its function is to allow a pilot to keep both hands on the controls while still communicating with those on the ground. In this case, controllers were able to overhear some of what was being said in the cockpit.

"The button was being pushed intermittently most of the way to New York," said one official later. "He wanted us to know something was wrong. When he pushed the button and the terrorist spoke, we knew. There was this voice that was threatening the pilot, and it was clearly threatening."[5]

Investigators strongly suspect that the pilot believed this hijacking would be similar to others that had occurred over the years: that he would be told to land the plane—perhaps at either

Kennedy or La Guardia Airport in New York—and the hijackers would make demands, using the passengers as hostages. During the overheard conversation, in fact, one of the terrorists told the pilot, "Don't do anything foolish. You're not going to get hurt."[6]

From the Back of the Plane

While the pilot was trying to keep the ground apprised of matters within the cockpit, one of the flight attendants used a cell phone to contact a supervisor back in Boston. The flight attendant, Madeline Amy Sweeney, hastily explained what was happening in the passenger sections. Later, investigators would give Sweeney credit for keeping her composure as she gave as much information as she could to the supervisor.

The terrorists, whom she described as Middle Eastern, had stabbed two of her fellow flight attendants and slit the throat of a passenger before storming the cockpit. The frightened passengers had been herded to the back of the plane, she said.

The Boston supervisor asked Sweeney if she had any idea of the new destination of the hijacked plane. She told him that it was clear the plane was dropping quickly, and said she was looking out a window at the time. She said, "I see water and buildings—Oh my God! Oh my God!"[7] At that point, say investigators, the transmission broke off as the aircraft slammed into the north tower of the World Trade Center.

An Easy Target

The World Trade Center, which was to be the target of the first two attacks on September 11, was a landmark—the most visible part of the New York skyline. Anyone who was lost momentarily could look up and get a sense of direction, since the towers were the easiest landmark to see. The Trade Center complex was made up of seven buildings, but the most well known were its giant twin towers—each 110 stories tall. Built in 1970, the World Trade Center had become a center of international finance and commerce.

Although the two towers were the tallest in New York City, the people of New York were less than enthusiastic about the World Trade towers. Many preferred the 1930s skyscrapers that had before made up New York City's impressive skyline—the Chrysler Building and the Empire State Building, for example. The World Trade Center, many thought, was just big, without much style. "No one loved it," wrote one New Yorker, "save children, who took to it because it was iconically simple, so tall and two. When a child tried to draw New York, he would draw the simplest available icons: two rectangles and an airplane going by them."[8]

The World Trade Center had been the target of terrorism before. In 1993, one thousand pounds of explosives were detonated in a van in an underground parking garage below the south tower. Six people were killed and over one thousand injured in that incident. However, the World Trade Center was quickly repaired, and with new security measures in place, the fifty thousand people who worked there each day felt that they were safe.

Too Horrible to Be Real

The impact of the aircraft hitting the north tower of the World Trade Center was sensed even before it was heard. Dogs lifted their heads, sensing danger. One man, fifteen blocks from the site, was startled by a huge flock of pigeons acting terrified for no apparent reason as they rose quickly into the air.

This happened just a second or two before he himself heard the crash.

The same delay occurred in office buildings near the World Trade Center. Several people in offices across the street felt a tremendous jolt and were thrown out of their chairs before they knew what was happening. One man who was in his car saw a huge wheel—which he later understood was from the airplane—fall from

The twin towers of the World Trade Center were easy targets. Each tower was 110 stories tall, the tallest buildings in New York City.

the sky onto a truck in front of him. He remembers how unreal it seemed.

Even to observers who saw the plane hit, the event seemed too horrible to be real. One man who was standing with a group of people saw the plane before it hit. "We all looked up," he says. "We all thought it would be unusual for a plane to be flying so low over the city. It scooped down even lower over the South Village—almost like a missile—and then toward the north tower.... When it went into the building, we all screamed—we couldn't believe what we saw." [9]

Disbelief instantly turned to panic for those who were in the north tower. The plane entered the building about twenty-five floors from the top. Many, of course, died instantly as the jet fuel from the aircraft exploded into a massive fireball. For others, death would come more slowly.

Thud

Those in the north tower below the crash floors quickly went to stairways to exit the building, which was rapidly becoming dark with smoke. Some were confused by the noise and bitter, greasy smoke that was laced with the strong fumes of jet fuel. Others who had been working at the World Trade Center in 1993 when it was bombed were quicker to react, and yelled instructions to coworkers, letting them know what to do.

"The World Trade Center"

Though the World Trade Center boasted the tallest towers on the New York skyline, many New Yorkers had disliked the building since it was completed in 1976, as poet David Lehman explains in his poem, "The World Trade Center," written after the bombing attempt in 1993. The poem was reprinted in "9.23.01: The Way We Live Now," in the New York Times Magazine, *September 23, 2001.*

I never liked the World Trade Center.
When it went up I talked it down
As did many other New Yorkers.
The twin towers were ugly monoliths
That lacked the details the ornament the
    character
Of the Empire State Building and especially
The Chrysler Building, everyone's favorite,
With its scalloped top, so noble.

The World Trade Center was an example
    of what was wrong
With American architecture.
And it stayed that way for twenty-five years
Until that Friday afternoon in February
When the bomb went off and the build-
    ings became
A great symbol of America, like the Statue
Of Liberty at the end of Hitchcock's
    "Saboteur."
My whole attitude toward the World Trade
    Center
Changed overnight. I began to like the way
It comes into view as you reach Sixth Avenue
From any side street, the way the tops
Of the towers dissolve into white skies
In the east when you cross the Hudson
Into the city across the George
    Washington Bridge.

Pedestrians look up in horror as a plane slams into the north tower.

Within a few minutes, the stairwells were filled with people making their way down. The building's electrical system quickly shut down, and those fleeing found themselves engulfed in total darkness. A few minutes later, automatic sprinklers came on, making the stairs slippery. One man who worked on the twentieth floor of the tower recalls urging on straggling coworkers who were having trouble breathing because of the smoke. Many of the women kicked off their shoes, realizing they could make better time without them.

However, even as people were groping through the dark stairways trying to get to safety, danger was imminent. The tower was groaning and rocking from the impact; steam pipes were bursting, and chunks of stone and plaster were raining down on those trying to flee. Many say that they were saying prayers as they moved down from one floor to another. "I never been to church since I was a kid,"

15

"I Got Lucky"

In the aftermath of the attacks, a number of stories were told of people who would almost certainly have died, were it not for some last-minute change in plans. This man, a janitor at the Trade Center, says it was a cup of coffee that saved him. This account was included in "Saving Grace," an article in People Weekly, *September 24, 2001.*

"My shift is 8 A.M. to 4:30 P.M. I'm always on time, but today I got lucky because I went on the 30th floor to get a cup of coffee. If I hadn't gotten that cup of coffee, I would have gotten blown up in the elevator. I was waiting by the elevator to go to the restrooms, and then there was a big bang, and the whole building shook. The elevator door flew open, and a guy stumbled out, and he was badly burned up. It seemed like he was smoldering, almost.

He was a delivery guy. The skin from his wrist was hanging down past his fingertips. He was screaming all sorts of things like, 'Bombing! Please get me out of here! I'm going to die!' I took him down the hallway right around the corner to my supervisor's office. Me and another janitor grabbed the man and took him outside, one on each arm. There was an EMS truck already outside, and those guys just grabbed him and pushed us aside. I wish I knew what happened to him, but I have no idea. He was burned up bad, but he was still alive. I really hope he survived."

---

admitted one man, "but you should have heard the Hail Marys I was saying. My old priest would have been surprised I even knew the words."[10]

A Blizzard of Paper

Those lucky enough to emerge from the north tower's lower floors found themselves in what one observer called "the mouth of Hell."[11] The scene outside was a flurry of ash and smoke. Broken glass was everywhere, and people were screaming and crying. Debris from above crashed on the sidewalks and streets below the tower. Subway passengers who had exited at the stop under the World Trade Center came up the stairs and into the daylight, "only to see plates of glass the size of store windows," writes one reporter, "and strips of metal larger than trucks flying out of buildings and plunging to the ground."[12]

One woman who had come down from the seventieth floor sobbed as she told of two coworkers who had been sucked out of their office window by gusts of wind, along with their desks and other furniture. And everywhere there was paper—a blizzard of work orders, memos, and spreadsheets from the various financial offices high above.

Saying Goodbye

Above the crash floors on the north tower, the scene was quite different. Although those working in offices near the top of the tower were unharmed, the aircraft had turned the floors below them into a superheated furnace, making escape impossible. Some remained confident, however, calling home on cell phones to reassure loved ones.

At 9:30 A.M., a man called home and left a message for his wife, Elizabeth. "Hi, hon. I'm OK. There was an explosion. I made it to the 78th floor. I'm helping people to get out; I'll see you soon." But as the minutes passed, the reality of their situation began to sink in. "My office is filled with smoke," a man on the 105th floor told his sister. "I can't see. Please tell the children I love them." [13]

The fire was spreading, closing in with flames and temperatures made much hotter because of the jet fuel. Many of the terrified workers held on to outside windows, trying to escape the heat and screaming for help as horrified spectators on the ground watched helplessly.

The Nightmare

Of all the remembrances of that morning, many say that the most vivid are those people who chose to jump from the top floors rather than die from the fire. "We watched as people jumped from the 90th floor," says one man who was working at a nearby building. "We saw a man and woman embrace, then jump together. We knew they had no chance. But I guess they figured they were going to die either way. Watching them, our hands shook. Our knees turned to jelly. My foreman was practically in tears." [14]

One man who lives thirteen blocks from the World Trade Center climbed onto his roof for a view of what was happening. He was skeptical when neighbors told him people were jumping from a hundred floors up:

I looked with my binoculars, and what they were saying were people was clearly debris—sheets of metal, chairs, unidentifiable stuff, and then a . . . oh God, a man in khakis and an open blue suit jacket, feet up in the air, falling down the side of the building facing the river,

Smoke billows from the north tower. The fire and smoke trapped many people on the floors above the impact.

17

three, four, five seconds, gone, vanished. … Then more people began to jump out the river side of the tower, and then out the front, where they fell against the backdrop of the windows, almost in sequence, like paratroopers bustling out of an aircraft.[15]

As long as she lives, says one young woman, she will never be able to get the grotesque images out of her mind—images of people so desperate that jumping was preferable to burning. "They had no chance of living. We watched them hit the ground, just landing on the street in front of us. . . . There was blood everywhere. . . . A young woman jumped out of a window who was wearing a red blouse and black skirt. I will be haunted by that image for the rest of my life. I could not watch any more."[16]

Flight 175

As Flight 11 was crashing into the north tower, another plane had been seized by hijackers. Like Flight 11, United Airlines

Spectators on the ground watch in disbelief as people began jumping from the tower to their deaths.

"The Birds Are on Fire"

As the following excerpt of an editorial from the September 18 edition of the New York Times *shows, schools that were extremely close to the World Trade Center were in session when the towers collapsed. It was only because of quick-thinking teachers that the students were evacuated safely.*

"The tragedy at the World Trade Center has produced scores of stories about people whose cool heads and courage saved lives. Among them are the public school teachers who evacuated several schools that were dangerously near the collapsing towers and moved a total of 8,000 children to safety without a single serious injury. Their achievement is all the more amazing given that the disaster struck on the third day of the school year, requiring many teachers to deal with frightened children whom they hardly knew....

The teachers at Public School 234, on Chambers Street, had to evacuate 6- and 7-year-olds during the most harrowing part of the disaster, just after the second trade center tower collapsed, enveloping the school in a debris-filled cloud.

Many of the children were screaming for parents who actually worked in the towers. As one teacher stepped into the street, a small child saw the burning bodies falling from the tower and cried out, 'Look, teacher, the birds are on fire!' Taking some students by the hand and carrying others on their shoulders, the teachers plunged through the rubble-strewn streets that were clogged with adults running for their lives. With their small charges in tow, they walked 40 minutes north to the safety of the nearest safe school in Greenwich Village. Some children whose parents could not get to them by the close of the day went home with teachers, with whom they stayed until their mothers or fathers could be reached by phone."

Flight 175 originated in Boston. Carrying fifty-six passengers and nine crew members, it, too, was on its way to Los Angeles. It was halfway between Newark and Philadelphia when it suddenly doubled back, toward New York City.

Investigators now believe that these hijackers had their own pilot, who took over the controls once the plane was in the air. Armed only with crude weapons such as plastic-handled box cutters, the terrorists are thought to have killed the pilot and crew. The passengers must have seen the skyline of the city to the left as they headed east, the skies now black with smoke from the north tower. One passenger, sensing what was to happen, called his parents on his cell phone, telling them, "I think we're going down, but don't worry. It's going to be quick."[17]

Newspaper and television crews, with their cameras already trained on the north tower, were in place at 9:06 A.M. as Flight 175 crashed into the south tower. Many watching the fiery impact on television believed at first that they were seeing footage of the first crash. However, the screams of the announcers soon made it clear that the image viewers were seeing was a second airplane that had just hit the World Trade Center.

The Second Attack

This plane came in lower, swooping in with its left wing banked, turning into the southeast corner of the south tower. One young man called his mother from the ninety-second floor, describing the plane he could see jutting out of the north tower, and the people he could see jumping to their deaths. "He sounded calm," a *Time* writer reports. "But suddenly he started screaming. He dropped the phone. His mother . . . held the line for half an hour, hoping he'd come back. He never did. Now she assumes her son was screaming at the sight of a plane heading toward his window." [18]

Those who had survived the crash emerged from the tower to a scene even more frenzied than it had been ten minutes before. On streets that were slick with blood, huge chunks of concrete, glass, and debris were crashing down, killing some rescue workers, crushing fire trucks and ambulances below—as though, say observers, those vehicles were toys. At least one firefighter was killed by a falling body.

Television cameras were already focused on the north tower when another plane appeared (left) and hit the south tower (right).

Above, in the tower, a fireball created by ten thousand gallons of jet fuel roared. Even so, as survivors were making their way out of the tower, firefighters and emergency medics were streaming in, ready to help the injured escape. Tragically, many of the rescuers would be dead within minutes.

"Straight Down Like an Elevator"

The towers had been built to withstand a great amount of wind—gales of up to two hundred miles per hour. And because the architects had been aware of the dangers inherent in one of the world's tallest structures, the buildings could even take a hit by a large airliner. However, the towers were not designed for the type of impact they suffered on September 11, 2001.

The burning jet fuel caused the fire in the towers to burn hotter than an ordinary fire. Because of where the aircraft hit the south tower, the tower's structural damage became evident first. The inner strength of the towers came from the steel girders—over 240 of them—which formed the perimeter of each floor. The girders on any floor were stress-bearing, meaning that they bore the weight of all of the floors above.

The heat, which was between one thousand and two thousand degrees, quickly began to affect the steel, making it as soft as modeling clay. "All that steel turns into spaghetti," explains one expert. "And then all of a sudden, that structure is untenable, and the weight starts bearing down on floors that were not designed to hold that weight, and you start having collapse." [19]

At 10:00 A.M. the south tower collapsed—straight down on top of itself. Pulitzer Prize–winning author John Updike was watching from a Brooklyn relative's roof when the tower collapsed. "As my wife and I watched . . . the south tower dropped from the screen of our viewing," he writes. "It fell straight down like an elevator, with a tinkling shiver and a groan of concussion distinct across the mile of air. We knew we had just witnessed thousands of deaths; we clung to each other as if we ourselves were falling." [20]

Outrunning the Cloud

The collapse created a thick cloud of concrete dust and glass, which seemed to gather momentum as it raced outward from the site through the canyons of lower Manhattan. Frightened people ran from it; those who could not outrun the cloud were either trampled or engulfed in unbreathable, dirty air. Most took off shirts or put scarves or handkerchiefs over their mouths and noses so they wouldn't suffocate from the dust.

One man recalls a police officer yelling for people to run, not walk—telling them that breathing the air would be fatal. Another man was leaving a nearby building amid a group of workers and found himself in the middle of a billowing cloud of ash:

> It was completely pitch black. You could not see your hands. I heard people bumping into people and falling and screaming for help. I was completely disoriented. I couldn't even tell which way was the sidewalk. I could see absolutely nothing. . . . My eyes were stinging so badly. I wandered around in the dark for

People run for their lives as the south tower collapses on top of itself spewing debris for blocks.

fifteen minutes and I was beginning to think I was going to die. I had trouble breathing. My eyes were closing. . . . Eventually a cop saw me and put me on a bus. I got off at about 32nd street on the East Side. I went to a pharmacy to get some drops for my eyes. The cashier looked at me and started to cry. [21]

"I Know They're Still in There"

The second tower collapsed twenty-nine minutes later, amid more smoke and debris.

Fires in both buildings continued to rage, and the sound of sirens was everywhere. The grim news was that few people were emerging from the ruins. Thousands, people speculated, had been trapped inside the towers when they fell. And unless they could be rescued quickly, most would surely die.

Firefighters especially were missing in large numbers. They had been on the scene early, and many were still inside when the towers collapsed. Entire squads were wiped out as they attended to the injured who were unable to evacuate the towers. By the end of the day, more than three hundred firefighters were either missing or known to be dead.

"These guys, they were heroes," sobbed a man who had escaped from the north tower. "They saved my life, they got me out of the stairway when it collapsed; they told me to run like hell out, toward the daylight. I thought I'd see them again, but I know they're still in there."[22]

Waiting for Bodies

As soon as the first plane hit, ambulances and emergency medical teams were assembled at the site. At first, they were extremely busy; many victims had received severe burns or had suffered broken bones or smoke inhala-tion. These patients were quickly taken to nearby hospitals. However, after the second plane and the subsequent collapses of the towers, area hospitals were alerted that they would soon be swamped with patients with severe injuries.

However, say medical technicians, hardly any patients were brought in after that first wave. In fact, the biggest problem wasn't shortages of bandages or morphine or other supplies—it was the overabundance of doctors, nurses, and volunteers. Ambulances from other areas of the city would pull up, sirens wailing, but with no one in the back. The drivers explained that they had come to help. And when they asked, "What can we do?" no one seemed to have an answer.

The second tower collapsed twenty-nine minutes after the first and the smoke and debris enveloped all of lower Manhattan.

Thousands of people walked for miles to escape the disaster.

One group of surgeons specializing in trauma were bused to the area to help. But it was clear, says Dr. Andrew Renner, that it was pointless. "This is a nightmare," he said. "We haven't seen any wounded. You're either going to walk out of there or you're dead."[23]

More Terror?

The long trails of people, shell-shocked and covered with ash, ran—and then walked— away from what had been the World Trade Center. The emergency medical people waited. And the firefighters and other rescue workers, grieving over friends that they knew had not come back out of the towers, frantically searched for survivors.

As all of these events were taking place, the rest of the nation was glued to television sets, horrified to learn that the tragedy in Manhattan was only part of the terror the United States was to experience that day.

Chapter Two

Two New Targets

Many who heard that the World Trade Center's north tower had been hit by a passenger jet assumed that it was a tragic accident, perhaps caused by a malfunctioning plane. However, with the arrival of a second suicide aircraft just minutes later, the truth was clear: America was under attack. And the attack was so well organized that two hijackings had occurred on the same morning, from the same airport.

The enemy—whoever they were—had chosen a very obvious symbol of U.S. business as their target. However, two more planes in the air had also been seized by hijackers. These two groups had targets other than business in mind.

Flight 77

About two hundred miles to the south of the crumbled towers in Manhattan, air traffic controllers at Dulles Airport outside Washington, D.C., had received a disturbing telephone call from U.S. solicitor general Theodore Olson. He had just been contacted by his wife, Barbara, a former federal prosecutor who had become a well-known television commentator during the impeachment hearings of Bill Clinton.

She was a passenger on American Airlines Flight 77, which had taken off from Dulles Airport and was en route to Los Angeles. She told her husband that the plane was being hijacked, and described how the terrorists had forced all the passengers to the rear of the plane. She also asked her husband what he thought the pilot should do. Before Olson could respond, however, the connection was broken.

The air traffic controllers had not received any information about a plane being hijacked from Dulles. Interestingly, however, several other families were getting cell phone calls from passengers on the flight, too. Investigators believe that those calls were not made secretly; it appears that the terrorists were encouraging passengers to call their loved ones, to let them know they were about to die.

Losing Contact

The air traffic controllers soon saw for themselves that something was happening on board Flight 77. The plane had gone westward for some distance into West Virginia before someone—presumably one of the hijackers—had turned off the plane's transponder, the device that transmits an airliner's speed and flight identification to controllers on the ground.

Now, with neither radio contact nor identification on their radar screen for Flight 77, ground control realized the plane had made a quick turnaround. It was now heading northeast, toward the Potomac River. With growing alarm, they saw that it was streaking into restricted airspace over the White House. For security purposes, no commercial or private aircraft are allowed to fly over certain U.S. buildings, such as the Capitol and the White House.

Hurriedly, ground control alerted the Secret Service of the security breach; although the president and his family were not in the White House at the time, many staff members were working in the West Wing. Secret

The White House was evacuated when it appeared to be the target of hijacked Flight 77.

The site of the third attack was the Pentagon when Flight 77 plowed into it thirty-three minutes after Flight 175 hit the second trade tower.

Service agents sent them running out of their offices to Pennsylvania Avenue.

A Military Target

But the plane's direction suddenly changed. "Just as [it] seemed to be on a suicide mission into the White House," writes one reporter, "the unidentified pilot executed a pivot so tight it reminded observers of a fighter jet maneuver."[24] The plane circled to the right and headed toward the Pentagon. It was flying so low at that point that it completely vanished from the radar screens.

One man driving nearby saw the jet swoop in, full throttle, its wings wobbling, flying no more than fifty feet off the ground. Another driver recalled the plane was extremely loud and was coming in so low that he could read the "AA" (for American

Airlines) on its side. Some firefighters working at the Pentagon's heliport heard the roar and looked up to see the plane—at this point only two hundred yards away. Still at full speed, it was only twenty-five feet off the ground and, they told one reporter, "was shearing off the tops of light poles and closing in like steel lightning."[25]

At 9:40 A.M. Flight 77 slammed into the southwest face of the Pentagon, the five-sided, five-story structure that is the headquarters of the five branches of the U.S. military. The jet rocked the building and ripped a gaping hundred-foot hole that extended from the ground to the roof.

No Match for a Suicide Crash

The twenty thousand employees—both civilian and military—at the Pentagon were already nervous. Like others throughout the nation, they had been watching the events at the World Trade Center. Some Pentagon employees, in fact, had even had a premonition that the Pentagon would be next.

The sixty-year-old Pentagon had been recently strengthened—ironically, in case of an enemy attack. Its concrete walls, two feet thick, were no match for a suicide crash, however. "All of a sudden," recalls one Pentagon worker, "there was this huge impact. I was thrown across my office. The floor buckled. The office filled with smoke. It was really terrifying." [26]

A man working on the helipad near the crash site agrees. Hearing the roar and feeling the fireball, he dove under a nearby van to escape the metal and other debris that exploded into the air. "Everything was on fire," he says. "The grass was on fire. The building was on fire. The firehouse was on fire." [27]

The crash killed all on board the plane, which disintegrated upon impact. Many inside the Pentagon were killed immediately, too—most by the fiery explosion. Officials say that the side that was hit houses the offices of army and navy operations personnel. No one could guess, when the crash occurred, how many people had actually been lost, but they knew it could have been worse. Because of the recent renovation many workers had not yet moved back into their offices.

"I Haven't Felt Something That Hot Before"

There was no shortage of rescue workers; at least one thousand firefighters, police, and Pentagon employees (many with combat experience) rushed to search for survivors. As at the World Trade Center, those rescue efforts were made extremely difficult by intense heat from the jet fuel.

One firefighter could not believe the intensity of the heat within the crash site. "We went into the building, searching for victims," he says. "There was so much fire, smoke, and damage. You couldn't see a lot, because of the smoke. It was dark, black smoke, and the walls were buckled out, and fire was balling down the hallway. . . . We were on the ground floor. I haven't felt something that hot before." [28]

One man was pinned down by fallen pipes, chunks of concrete, and furniture. To allow them time to remove the debris, rescuers formed chains, passing wet T-shirts to one another to protect their faces from the smoke. "It took 30 men 30 minutes to get just that one guy to the door 15 feet away," says one rescue worker. "That heat and fire—it could eat you alive in three seconds." [29]

Also similar to the crisis in New York City, very few victims were being taken to hospitals. As soon as the crash occurred, hospitals throughout northern Virginia and Washington, D.C., were put on high alert—that they should expect a heavy influx of ambulances.

Only seventy patients were treated at those hospitals, however. Many had severe burns over half of their bodies; other patients had serious lung trouble from smoke inhalation. Most in the vicinity of the blast died immediately—or at least before rescuers could reach them. There were exceptions thanks to heroic rescue efforts.

A Human Chain

Lieutenant Colonel Marilyn Wills had been knocked across the room on the second floor where she had been working. The room was black, and she could hear screams as she crawled in search of a doorway. One woman nearby was frozen with fear—unable to move. Wills told the woman to hold on to her pant leg, and they crawled together. They came across another woman—an officer—and Wills added her to the chain.

However, once they found the door and got out into the hallway, they encountered more problems. Not only did the exits appear blocked with debris, the two women Wills was helping were overcome with smoke, as one reporter writes:

> [The] officer started choking. The sprinklers had cut on, and Wills's sweater was as waterlogged as a sponge. "Put the sweater over your mouth and suck the water out!" Wills ordered. The civilian on the back of the chain called out that she couldn't make it. Wills shoved the sweater into her face, too. When Wills turned around, the woman in front was

"The Pentagon Has Been Hit!"

In this excerpt from "Crisis Management," which appears in People Weekly, *Mike Walter, a correspondent from* USA Today Live Television *recalls how terrified he was when the plane crashed into the Pentagon.*

"This morning the traffic near the Pentagon was just crawling along. I looked out the window and saw a plane coming over, loud and very low. I could read the 'AA' on its side. It looked like it was 20, 30 feet up in the air. It was coming in a direct path to the Pentagon. I started to say to myself, 'This plane is going to crash.' It disappeared behind the trees, and there was a massive explosion. I kept muttering, 'Ohmigod, ohmigod.' It was surrealistic. The traffic had stopped. A woman was screaming, 'Turn around, turn around! The Pentagon has been hit!' It was just pandemonium.

I pulled over and ran to see what I could see. There was debris from the jet on the overpass. I was watching the military personnel set up a triage. These tarps, red and green and yellow. And flags. They were running around with stretchers. All of a sudden they grabbed them and started running for the Pentagon. Three or four military officers came running up saying, 'You've got to get back! Another plane's been hijacked and is heading our way!' People were saying it was 25 minutes away, others said 25 miles away. Then an F-16 came screaming by the Pentagon, and people cheered. There was a staff sergeant standing next to me saying, 'What do they do if it's a passenger plane and they shoot it down?' I tried to stay busy, tried to work [filing television reports]. When all this was over, an Army guy came over and said, 'The FBI wants to talk to you.' I dissolved into tears. He said, 'Don't worry about it. You're in a state of shock.'

Psychologically, this is pretty jarring. So often [reporters] show up, and the yellow tape is up, and it's after the fact. To be there and watch it was very tough."

gone. Crawling again, she saw a pin of light down the corridor—a window. A soldier was breaking it with a fax machine. Reaching him, Wills found the strength to stand, and helped lower her civilian companion and another woman two stories to rescuers below. Wills said she was going back for the officer from her human chain. A colonel, pushed back by the billowing smoke looked at her. "No," he said.[30]

Shutdown

Those who were able to evacuate the building milled around outside, where military helicopters circled the surrounding area, looking for another air assault. Many raced to the Pentagon's day care facility to make sure their children were safe. The children had been evacuated to a grassy area nearby and were unaware of what was happening around them.

As hundreds of rescue vehicles raced to the Pentagon, the federal government closed its offices. More than 250,000 people left hurriedly, not knowing what to expect. Their hurried departure, in addition to the closing of downtown businesses, made traffic impossible. On the nearly empty streets around the Capitol, hundreds of National Guard members patroled in humvees.

A rescue helicopter flies over the Pentagon. Flight 77 ripped a one-hundred-foot hole in the southwest face of the building.

Just as the World Trade Center was a symbol of American business and financial affairs, the Pentagon was an obvious symbol, too. Never before had it been attacked, and to many Americans, seeing its one side crumbled and burning seemed almost impossible to believe. One man, whose office was destroyed, sadly recalled that just the day before, he had looked out his window to see President Bush taking off from the helipad, now in ruins.

"You couldn't feel that there was any safer place in the world," he said. "After my home, I viewed my office as the most secure place I could be."[31]

Flight 93

Unbelievably, a fourth airplane was hijacked that same morning. United Airlines Flight 93 took off from Newark International Airport and was bound for San Francisco. That aircraft, and the thirty-eight passengers and seven crew members it carried, became highly important for what *did not* occur on it, rather than what did. Unlike those on the other three airplanes, the terrorists on board Flight 93 did not accomplish their deadly mission. It is almost certain that a few very brave passengers saved hundreds of lives on the ground that morning.

The airplane was to have taken off at 8:01 A.M., but was forty minutes late. It was just south of Cleveland, Ohio, when it took a sudden, sharp left turn and headed back toward Pennsylvania. Ground control, fearful of what was happening to Flight 93, tried to contact the crew by radio, but without success.

Soon afterward, air traffic controllers in Cleveland picked up a radio signal from the plane. Although the transmission was somewhat muffled, controllers did hear screams, then silence, and then more screams. They also heard the words "Bomb on board." By this time, both towers of the World Trade Center in New York were in flames, and Barbara Olson was in the process of telling her husband of her flight's hijacking. What was happening to Flight 93?

A Flurry of Phone Calls

Soon after the alarming radio transmission, some of Flight 93's passengers were making cell phone calls of their own—to family members. Days later, these phone calls were able to give investigators a much clearer understanding of what actually happened on that flight.

Some callers described the hijackers as Arab or from the Middle East. The three men, they said, wore red headbands. The men, they said, were carrying knives, and one had a box with red markings that the hijackers said was a bomb. After the hijackers took control of the plane, a man with an Arabic accent announced, "This is the captain speaking. Remain in your seat. There is a bomb on board. Stay quiet. We are meeting with their demands. We are returning to the airport."[32]

Perhaps if the plane had taken off on time, the passengers would have had no reason to doubt the announcement—that the plane would land safely and no harm would come to them if demands were met—but the fact that the airplane had taken off forty minutes late would end up making a huge difference.

"So Armed, They Could Act"

In this excerpt from his Time *magazine editorial "The Greater the Evil, the More It Disarms," Charles Krauthammer asks—and answers—the question: Why were the passengers of Flight 93 the only ones who fought back against the hijackers?*

"The passengers' seeming passivity is reminiscent of the Holocaust. We ask, with trepidation: How could Jews have allowed themselves to be herded into gas chambers by just a few people carrying machine guns? Because it was inconceivable—that the men carrying the weapons would do what they, in fact, did do. The victims were told these were showers. Who could imagine herding children into gas chambers? In all of history, no people had ever done that. The victims could not plumb the depths of their enemy's evil.

I suspect the same thing happened to the doomed passengers on the hijacked planes.

After all, hijackings had been going on for 40 years. Almost invariably, everybody ends up OK.... Never in history had hijackers intentionally turned a passenger plane into a flying bomb, killing everyone aboard, including themselves. Decades of experience teach us that if you simply do what the hijackers say, they'll eventually get tired and give up. That's the rule.

But when the rules don't apply, when inconceivably cold-blooded evil is in command, the victims are truly helpless.... Why then did the passengers on the plane that went down near Pittsburgh decide to resist the hijackers and prevent them from completing their mission? Because they knew: their relatives had told them by cell phone that the World Trade Center had already been attacked by hijacked planes. They were armed with final awareness of the nature of the evil they faced.

So armed, they could act. So armed, they did."

"The Passengers Wouldn't Have Had the Big Picture"

At least one passenger had heard the fate of the two hijacked planes that had crashed into the World Trade Center, and he shared that information with some of his fellow passengers. That knowledge would have given passengers on Flight 93 a more accurate idea of what was probably going to be their fate, too. Says one Defense Department official, "It would have changed the events if the plane had taken off on time. The passengers wouldn't have had the big picture. They would have been dealing only with the misinformation supplied by the hijackers."[33]

The passenger who first learned about the crisis in New York City was Tom Burnett, an executive with a medical device company in California. He had called his wife, Deena, and told her his plane had just been hijacked and that the men had knifed one of the passengers. He gave her the flight number and told her to call the authorities. It was then that Deena gave him the disturbing news about the other hijackings.

After awhile, Burnett called her back with a very sobering announcement. "I know we're all going to die," he said. "There's three of us that are going to do something about it."[34] Deena says, "I pleaded with him to please sit down and not draw attention to himself," she said later. "And he said, 'No, no. If they're going to run this into the ground we're going to have to do something.' And he hung up," she says, "and never called back."[35]

"Let's Roll"

Soon afterward, Lyzbeth Glick received a cell phone call from her husband, Jeremy. He, too, was on Flight 93 and wanted to know if it was true—that people had crashed planes into the World Trade Center. His wife confirmed the grim news. Glick told her what

Tom Burnett had told his wife—that several of the passengers were going to take a vote on how to proceed, but he thought they would take on the hijackers. He even joked, she said, that they would use the butter knives from the in-flight breakfast.

Another passenger, thirty-one-year-old Mark Bingham, called his mother with much of the same information. During the call, his mother could hear him talking in the background, talking quietly with others about their plans. His mother has no doubt that he would have fought against the terrorists.

Todd Beamer could not reach his wife on the plane's in-flight phone because it rejected his credit card. He was routed to an

Todd Beamer (in picture frame) perished on Flight 93. He leaves behind two sons David (left) and Andrew, and wife Lisa. Lisa is pregnant with the couple's third child.

operator supervisor instead. He told her of the hijacking and how some of the passengers were going to fight back. He also gave the operator his home phone number, and asked her to call his wife and tell her how much he loved her and his two little boys. The last thing the operator heard was, "Are you ready, guys? Let's roll." [36]

Screams and Silence

At least one of the cell phones was left on after that. Law enforcement officers who had been alerted to the hijacking were listening in on Jeremy Glick's last call to his wife. After he finished talking, they could hear screams in the background and then silence.

The plane's cockpit recorder later gave a more vivid look at the plane's final minutes. Investigators say that scuffling sounds and shouting were heard in both Arabic and English. Writes one reporter, "Investigators are operating on the theory that the men somehow made their way up 100 feet from the rear of the plane into the cockpit. The cockpit voice recorder indicates someone, probably a hijacker, screaming, 'Get out of here. Get out of here.' Then grunting, screaming, and scuffling. Then silence." [37]

What happened then is much more evident. Investigators say that it is almost certain that because of that struggle, Flight 93 went down very quickly. Eyewitnesses near the

Investigators search the crash site of Flight 93, the only hijacked plane that missed its target.

crash site, which was a coalfield in western Pennsylvania, said that the plane flew low and suddenly fell from the sky. Some said it was making a whistling sound, like a missile.

One witness, who was sitting on his porch less than one-quarter mile from the crash site, commented that the plane had seemed to fall straight down, like a stone. Another man rushed to the site, hoping he could help somehow. However, there was little evidence of a plane, let alone survivors. The plane, at almost full throttle, had made a ten-by-twenty-foot crater in the field and was reduced to charred fragments.

A Lone Bright Spot

Investigators have uncovered another important piece of information. Because of the struggle and subsequent crash, the terrorists on the plane were not able to carry out their assigned mission—a suicide crash, just as terrorists on the other three hijacked planes had done. Investigators are almost certain the plane had reversed its direction to fly to Washington, D.C. The specific target, they say, was most likely the White House or the Capitol.

Though Flight 93 had crashed and all aboard were killed, the heroics on board would later prove to be one of the only bright spots in a time of unspeakable tragedy. But on September 11, after the four hijacked planes had crashed, after the Pentagon had been attacked and the World Trade Center demolished, there was little time to reflect on heroism or what might have been. Immediate concerns needed to be addressed: searching for possible survivors, putting out the fires that still smoldered in Washington, D.C. and New York, and wondering if other deadly attacks were coming.

Chapter Three

A Nation Reacts

As the emergency workers—fire-fighters, police, and medical personnel—were reacting to the attacks at the World Trade Center and the Pentagon, another level of activity was much less visible. It was clear that the nation had been attacked, but no one knew if these four hijacked planes were just the beginning of a flurry of terrorist strikes on American targets. And because no one was sure, tightening national security as quickly as possible was critical.

The Commander in Chief

At the time the World Trade Center was being attacked, President George W. Bush was in Sarasota, Florida, sitting in front of a second grade classroom in Emma E. Booker Elementary. He had come to talk to children about education and was listening as some of the excited seven-year-olds were reading aloud for him, when an aide came into the room and whispered something to the president.

Bush's face became very serious; however, he remained in the room for a few minutes more—although teachers say he was obviously distracted by what he had heard. The president listened as the last little boy finished reading aloud. "Really good readers, whew!" he told them. "These must be sixth graders." [38] He quickly left the classroom and, after speaking to school officials for a few minutes, the president and his aides boarded *Air Force One* for Washington, D.C.

Decisions from *Air Force One*

The heightened security resulted in a very roundabout trip back to the White House. On *Air Force One*, which had been vigorously searched and researched for explosives, Bush was in contact with Vice President Dick Cheney in Washington about the most recent developments, such as the plane crash at the Pentagon. Cheney, who had been rushed to a safe location on the grounds of the White House by the Secret Service, discussed with the president the order that all airplanes over the United States must land immediately. After all, no one knew how many more of the hijacked planes were on their way to targets. The two men discussed how to deal with a plane that did not comply with landing orders. The military, Bush finally decided, would have to shoot down that plane—an incredibly wrenching decision. (Since all planes did comply, it was an order that did not have to be carried out.)

Cheney also urged Bush to delay coming to Washington and to fly instead to a secure military base. A few bases are designed especially for times such as these—when the country is under attack and the president's life

President Bush learns of the terrorist attacks on the World Trade Center.

might be in jeopardy. One base is in Nebraska, and Bush's Secret Service agents decided that he should go there until the situation seemed safe.

Defcon Delta

However, Bush and his aides also knew that it was very important for the nation to hear from him so that the American people would know that their government was still functioning. En route to the base in Nebraska, *Air Force One* stopped at an air force base in Louisiana so that the president could make a short speech. The situation at the base was tense as soldiers in full combat array stood guard. The nation was at Defcon Delta—the code name for the highest state of national alert.

Bush's speech was terse. "Freedom itself was attacked this morning by a faceless coward, and freedom will not be defeated," he said. "Make no mistake: the United States will hunt down and punish those responsible for these cowardly acts."[39] After his speech, Bush consulted with military advisers at the base, and not until that night did he finally get home to the White House.

Some criticized the president, accusing him of hiding when the American people needed him most. However, historian David McCullough explained that President Bush had little to say about the precautions that were taken: "All presidents do what they're told on matters of personal security," he said. "The most important thing is that the president is alive and safe and knows what's going on. We haven't seen this level of destruction on our home ground since the Civil War. This isn't the 'Titanic' movie. It's real."[40]

Shutting Down

With the president's safety assured, other important security measures could be taken. All air traffic had been suspended—something that had never before happened in the United States. This meant, too, that airliners en route to the United States from Europe and Asia had to be diverted to Canada. At airports throughout North America, passengers stranded far from home waited anxiously for word of resumed flights.

In New York City, the New York Stock Exchange was closed—hardly a surprise, since it is so close to the site of the World Trade Center. The navy sent two aircraft carriers—the USS *John F. Kennedy* and the *George Washington*—to patrol off New York harbor. F-16s prowled the skies over Washington, New York, and other large cities. Bridges and tunnels into Manhattan were closed.

Broadway, with its multitude of theaters, was dark, and major league baseball was canceled for the first time since D-Day, the Allied invasion of Europe during World War II. Any attraction or building that could possibly be thought of as a target for terrorists was closed: Chicago's Sears Tower, Disneyland and Walt Disney World, Minnesota's Mall of America, the Seattle Space Needle, Mount Rushmore, and even Independence Hall, the Philadelphia shrine where the Liberty Bell is displayed.

Continuing to Search at Ground Zero

As security measures tightened nationwide, hopeful rescuers were still combing the rubble of the World Trade Center. Though it seemed less and less likely, they still hoped to find someone alive. Firefighters, police officers, and others who had not perished in the collapse were now digging through the ashy debris at what was now being called Ground Zero. Because fires were still raging beneath the ruins, the footing was still extremely hot in many places, and firefighters' boots, despite rubber soles four inches thick, were actually melting to their feet.

They found some bodies, including what appeared to be people strapped into airplane seats, as well as the body of a flight attendant with her hands bound. One firefighter admitted that he had to stop working for a little while after finding the body of a baby strapped in her car seat. The car had been knocked over by falling debris from the south tower.

However, most of what rescue workers found were parts of bodies. During the first week, rescuers just marked such remains, but kept digging. Finding a person still alive would have to take precedence, at least until it was clear that hope had run out.

Eventually the remains were retrieved and were put in individual body bags. Rescuers would take the bags out to refrigerated trucks, which would take them to the morgues. New York mayor Rudolph Giuliani ordered thirty thousand additional body bags when it became apparent how extensive the loss of life was—and how scattered the remains.

New York City Fire Department personnel work in a bucket brigade at Ground Zero.

Discouraged Dogs

Special dog teams, known as the K-9 squad, were brought to the site, too. Each dog works with a police officer and alerts its handler when it sniffs out the presence of a living person. Between two hundred and three hundred dogs and their handlers from all over the United States helped at Ground Zero, but with almost no success.

One disappointed handler said that he and his dog Gus found many body parts, but no living people. Gus, like most other dogs in K-9 units, is trained to sit down as soon as he smells a person. However, after working for several ten- to twelve-hour shifts, Gus had found nothing at all. Some on the scene said that the mountains of ash that cover everything may have interfered with the dogs' sensitive noses. Others believe that there was simply too much death—the smell of too much flesh was overpowering the dogs' sense of smell.

The search was as dangerous for the dogs as it was for any other rescue workers. Vets at the scene routinely treated dogs for dehydration and burning eyes. Many of the dogs were plagued by burns on their paw pads. Many had bloody paws from hours walking through sharp debris, too. (Some volunteers sewed more than fifteen hundred heavy-duty dog boots to allow the dogs to keep working without risking more serious injuries.)

However, the biggest toll on the K-9 units was discouragement. One trainer whose dog emerged from the debris with a torn, scorched teddy bear in its mouth, explained that his dog was not accustomed to going so long without success. To keep the dogs focused after hours of fruitless searching, trainers would take turns hiding under blankets and letting other trainers' dogs find them. "These dogs are trained to find live people," said an emergency care veterinarian. "It's positive energy for them—but they're finding just cadavers and body parts. The handlers try to stay upbeat, because the dogs take their cues from them, even though [the handlers] are very upset and moved to tears. Besides veterinary attention, we also give them affection—the handlers are bringing dogs back to get cuddled." [41]

A Moment of Silence

The rescuers were discouraged, too. Among the firefighters especially, the realization of how many of their coworkers had been lost began to sink in. Firefighters think of themselves as a true brotherhood; when one of their own dies, it is as painful as losing a family member. With three hundred firefighters lost and presumed dead, the grief, said those on the scene at Ground Zero, was immense.

That is why, when a firefighter's body was found, everyone paused for a moment of silence. "All the machinery is turned off," explained one firefighter, "and everybody takes their helmets off while a body bag is brought over and brothers from his station come and carry him away." [42]

The people of New York City were extremely supportive. Many brought casseroles and baked goods to the station houses. One visitor was amazed at the ability of the firefighters to cope with the nightmarish scenes they witnessed each day at Ground Zero. She

President George Bush comforts a firefighter during his tour of Ground Zero. More than three hundred New York City firefighters lost their lives when the towers collapsed.

said, "They're made of something I've not seen before."[43]

The station houses became shrines, decorated with votive candles, pictures, flowers, and letters from the neighborhood. One note, from a ten-year-old, was especially touching to the rescuers: "I am so sorry you lost your best friends. I hope you will be all right and you will not lose your lives. Be safe and wear heavy equipment."[44]

Waiting

As the rescue workers searched, family members of those missing since September 11 watched from a distance. They had no way of knowing whether their loved ones had been found and taken to a hospital, or had been found dead, or had not been found at all. In the first forty-eight hours, those in New York made posters with a photograph of their loved

41

So Many Funerals

The huge number of deaths in New York City resulted in such a steady stream of funerals there that many people were overwhelmed. In this excerpt from her article "The Circles of Loss," New York's Jennifer Senior relates how difficult it is for some communities to cope.

"Mass death has the curious effect of both magnifying a person's importance and trivializing it. These funerals and memorials, traditionally intimate rituals, have become epic events, as public as the deaths of the victims themselves. Last Tuesday, 1,300 people descended on the Church of the Resurrection in Larchmont for the memorial of Frank McGuinn, a managing director at Cantor Fitzgerald [a company whose staff was almost completely wiped out in the attacks]; the family needed six condolence books.

On Thursday, Christine Bennett had a funeral for her fiance, Danny Rosetti, who perished while installing office furniture for AON on the 105th floor of Tower Two. She felt like half the town of Bloomfield, New Jersey, showed up. 'Our escort—there had to be at least ten police cars out in front with their sirens going,' she says. . . . These mass outpourings are, of course, stunning tributes to the dead. But they are also forums for collective grieving; they have become a means for people to work through the events of September 11, even if they were not directly affected.

Ed Fox, director of John J. Fox Funeral Home in Larchmont—his town lost at least three—wonders whether these giant ceremonies tend to drown out the needs of the people closest to the deceased. Some families, he says, took to putting up signs on their front doors last week—firm but polite notes thanking their neighbors for stopping by but further explaining: 'We're not receiving people today.'

'The families appreciate all the support,' says Fox. 'But they've had to limit contact with people. So much support can become counterproductive.'"

ones, with the words "Have you seen . . . ?" and "Please call this number" scrawled on the bottom.

The posters were taped or stapled to every window, every telephone pole, outside every hospital emergency room door. Posters were pinned to the chests of the family members, too. And they walked from hospital to hospital, hoping someone would recognize the photograph on their chests, hoping for news. Every so often, there would be a rumor—a cell phone ringing far beneath the rubble, or a story that a policeman trapped underneath fired his gun to alert rescuers. Such rumors got people excited for a short time, but eventually proved to be false.

In the days and weeks that followed without news, families were asked to fill out long questionnaires. They were asked about the dental records, scars, tattoos, and jewelry of the missing and the dead. Blood relatives could provide DNA samples—a swab from the inside of their cheeks, usually—along with the victim's toothbrush or razor. These items would help medical examiners match up the remains brought in from the Pentagon, the

World Trade Center, or the Pennsylvania crash site with the correct family.

"I Just Don't Know What Else to Do"

The reaction of the medical community, the rescuers, the military, and various governmental agencies was extremely important in dealing with the aftermath of the September 11 attacks. However, many American people not in uniform reacted in important ways, too.

Many gave blood—in fact, Red Cross officials were astonished soon after they put out an appeal for donors. They had so many people responding that they had to turn some

A man is overwhelmed as he reads the many missing person notices attached to a tree in New York City.

away. In New York, the line of donors at the Blood Center—more than a thousand people—extended almost around a full block. "It's just amazing," said one nurse standing in the donors' line. "There'll be a three- or four-hour wait, and just look at all of these people standing here."[45]

A lot of those who waited in line said they wanted to do something to help, but were not sure what. One man in a San Francisco blood bank was nervously waiting for word of a New York friend who was missing after the attacks. "I'd keep giving blood if I had enough," he said. "I just don't know what else to do."[46]

Doughnuts, Dancing, and Virtual Kool-Aid

Many people watching the events on television felt the same way—as though they, too, wanted to help in some way. "Seeing people racing through the streets in Manhattan without shoes, just tearing away as fast as they could go—that did it for me," recalled one Minnesota woman emotionally. "I was watching on TV—people with soot and ash all over them, bleeding, crying. I felt like, hey, this is my country; and those are my people going through hell. And I'm sitting

Wanting to help, people lined up for blocks in cities around the United States to donate blood.

"The End of the Free Ride"

Although many nations around the world sent sympathy and pledged support soon after the attacks, some nations' responses were seen as lukewarm, and were unclear about how much support they would offer. In this excerpt from his Newsweek *editorial "The End of the End of History," Fareed Zakaria notes that there are places throughout the world that are not supportive enough of the United States—but the effects of the terrorism of September 11 will soon convince them that without a secure America, they will eventually suffer, too.*

"For America, this is the end of unilateralism. And for the rest of the world it is the end of the free ride. People are now going to realize just how much they enjoyed the benefits of globalization; the peace and prosperity; the ease of trade and travel, the information and entertainment. They watched the movies, listened to the music, read the magazines, vacationed in America, and sent their children to college here. But none of this required them actively to support the United States or affirm its values. They could denounce America by day and consume its bounties by night.

But all these countries—in Europe and Asia and Latin America—must recognize that the world they have gotten used to will not survive if America is crippled. The United States is the pivot that makes today's globalization go round. If other countries believe in individual liberty, in free enterprise and free trade, in religious freedom, in democracy, then they are eating the fruits of the American order. And this order can be truly secure only when all those who benefit from it stand in its defense. Those abroad who love liberty cannot watch this war as if it were a horror movie, wondering how it will end. This is your struggle, too."

here, feeling like I want to connect, you know?"[47]

A lot of Americans felt the same way. "It was clear," wrote columnist Nancy Gibbs soon after the attacks, "that people ached to live bigger lives, to find some way to be a brave and generous part of what most of us were consigned to watch only on television."[48] Some mobilized their church or civic group and collected funds for the victims and their families. Some opened their homes to travelers stranded at a nearby airport.

In Washington, several people bought huge quantities of bottled water and handed it out to rescuers. An air force major who had survived the Pentagon attack was deeply moved by an experience he had several days afterward. He had gone to a coffee shop near his office. The shop owner told him he didn't have to pay—that a woman had come by earlier and given a lot of money to pay the bill of any soldier that came in.

"The woman who gave [the shop owner] the money had just lost her husband or son in the disaster at the Pentagon," said the major. "This poor woman should have been in deep mourning. Instead, she's buying coffee and doughnuts for us guys in uniform. I have no answers to how someone cultivates a heart as large as that."[49]

Children, too, wanted to help—and found creative ways to show their support for America. One kindergartner in New Jersey renamed all of her dolls George Bush. A Texas eight-year-old sold her drawings as well as virtual cups of Kool-Aid on eBay to raise money for the victims. A six-year-old girl who was taking Irish step dance lessons set up a card table outside her North Carolina home with a poster decorated with Irish and American flags, urging people to contribute money to help the victims. As an incentive, she danced on the sidewalk nearby.

Helping

The grounding of all the nation's airplanes provided two young Dallas men with an opportunity to help. Matthew Harris and Eddie Perryman, who recover and process human tissue for the University of Texas Southwestern Medical Center, were watching the rescue efforts on television. They knew that many of the survivors, especially those who escaped from the crash at the Pentagon, were burn victims who would need skin grafts.

Since the normal way of transporting tissue or organs in emergencies—by airplane—was no longer an option, the two men volunteered to drive seventy square feet of skin for grafts to Washington in three large Styrofoam coolers. It was a frantic drive, for the sensitivity of the tissue made time an important factor. Even so, the men were glad to have contributed. Shrugged Harris, "We jumped at the opportunity."[50]

In New York City, enormous support was shown not only for the victims but also for the ever-present rescue workers. Many brought snacks and other things to the site for the workers. Long display tables were brought out from several nearby stores, and they were laden with everything from brownies and fresh fruit to aspirin and boxes of clean socks.

One resident smiles as he recalls some of the people who were so eager to help:

> A woman came with lunch bags, like my mother used to make. You know, a brown paper bag with a peanut-butter-and-jelly sandwich, a candy bar, and a folded napkin. A hundred of them. A guy came down … in his wheelchair and said, "Please, please, please take the bag in back of me. I made these sandwiches—would you give them to the men?" It's just mind-blowing.[51]

Down Time

For many Americans, no matter where they lived, the reactions to the tragedy were very personal and very private. Throughout the nation, families and friends scrambled to connect with one another. "My mom and I don't always get along, but she was the first person I wanted to call," said one twenty-three-year-old. "She lives up north, and I tend not to call her too often, because we end up fighting about something. But it didn't seem that important on the eleventh."[52]

"I just wanted to make sure my kids knew I love them," said one woman. "I wanted to physically just touch them, and make sure they were all right. It's a feeling I haven't had since they were really little, you know? When they're newborns, and you look at them and think how little and vulnerable they are? That's how I think now."[53]

Horrific images like this one motivated people around the country to help the victims in any way they could.

Many people also found comfort in finding a quiet place to think. Churches, synagogues, and temples stayed open for people who wanted to pray, light a candle, or just reflect on what had happened. Some organized candlelight vigils and were amazed at both the numbers and the variety of people who attended.

As varied as the responses and reactions were—whether one chose to meditate, bake cookies, give blood, or simply watch the continuous television coverage—everyone seemed to share one reaction. After the shock and the horror of seeing the nation attacked in such a way, one word summed up the question on the minds of most people: *Who?*

Chapter Four

Looking for Answers

After the second plane, United Flight 175, slammed into the the south tower of the World Trade Center, it was clear that these crashes were not accidental—the result of pilot error or a mechanical malfunction. These were acts of terrorism, violence committed to further a political, social, or religious cause by frightening and victimizing innocent people.

Terrorists by definition are not an army of any nation; they usually consist of small groups who do their killing suddenly and secretively. As was the case in the attacks of September 11, terrorists frequently target civilians.

Proceed Cautiously

Many terrorists exist around the world—including some in the United States. President Bush knew it was important that Americans not jump to conclusions about who had committed the suicide crashes. The nation had learned that lesson after the bombing of the federal building in Oklahoma City, Oklahoma, in 1995.

After that blast, which killed 168 people, many reporters and investigators quickly assumed that those responsible were Middle Eastern terrorists. It was perhaps an understandable presumption, for only two years before, Middle Eastern terrorists had attempted to destroy the World Trade Center by parking a truck laden with explosives in the lower parking garage. However, the Oklahoma bombing was homegrown terrorism, as the nation found out. Two former U.S. soldiers who hated the government, Timothy McVeigh and Terry Nichols, were convicted of the crime.

Had Americans been behind the terrorism of September 11 as well? It was obvious that the United States had been singled out by terrorists who were willing to die during the course of their attacks. Who were they?

Well Funded and Well Planned

Violent American right-wing groups were eliminated quickly; the cell phone messages from passengers on at least one of the hijacked flights described the men as Arab or Middle Eastern. Also, ground control was able to hear that it was a man with an Arabic accent who made an announcement on Flight 93 before it crashed.

Islamic extremist Osama bin Laden quickly became a suspect.

Palestinian terrorists were a possibility. The United States has long been a strong supporter of Israel, against whom Palestinians have been fighting for years. Militant Palestinians often plan and carry out suicide bombings in crowded Israeli market places and streets. Iraq, too, was a possibility. Saddam Hussein, Iraq's leader, had been a sworn enemy of the United States since before the Persian Gulf War. Although Iraqi or Palestinian groups might have had motive, American intelligence sources did not believe that either would have had the resources to conduct an operation as large as that of September 11.

In fact, no terrorist group except one had ever demonstrated what one reporter calls "the will, wallet, or gall to attack the U.S. before."[54] That one was the network known as al-Qaeda, which is a loose-knit group of terrorists controlled by Osama bin Laden—a Saudi Arabian–born Islamic extremist who is known to have trained thousands.

"It Is Something We Wish For"

From the beginning, evidence seemed to point to bin Laden. For one thing, he had targeted the United States before. He was responsible for the 1998 bombing of U.S. embassies in Tanzania and Kenya, which killed 224 people. Terrorists linked to Osama bin Laden were also responsible for the bombing of the USS *Cole* in Yemen in 2000—an attack that killed 17.

In an interview with an Arab journalist less than a month before the September attacks, bin Laden mentioned a new, unprecedented attack that he was planning against the United States. He had never been reluctant to express his hate for Americans—or "infidels," as he called them. He saw the United States as a place of wickedness and corruption, and stated that it was a holy duty for Muslims to kill Americans—civilians included.

"Being killed for Allah's cause is a great honor achieved by only those who are the elite of the nation," he told CNN reporters in 1997. "We love this kind of death for Allah's cause as much as you like to live. We have nothing to fear for. It is something we wish for." [55]

The magnitude of the attack—the planning and coordination required to pull it off— pointed to bin Laden, too. An extremely wealthy man—estimates are that he had access to at least $250 million—he was more than capable of funding projects that might take months or even years of preparation. By the evening of September 11, investigators at the National Security Agency found evidence to further back up what investigators had supposed. They intercepted two electronic messages—apparently from other al-Qaeda operatives within the United States—that were being sent to bin Laden. The messages stated simply, "We have hit the targets." [56]

Operation PENTTBOMB

Soon after the September 11 attacks, the Federal Bureau of Investigation (FBI) launched a major investigation. Like all Bureau investigations, it had a code name—PENTTBOMB, for Pentagon Twin Towers Bombings. One goal of PENTTBOMB investigators was to systematically follow the trail of evidence until they could prove who committed the actions and with whom they were

working. The second and more urgent goal was to find out whether more terrorist strikes were planned.

It was probably the largest FBI operation in history. More than seven thousand agents worked with thousands of state and local agencies to follow an overwhelming 63,232 leads in the first week after the attacks. By the following week, the number of leads had ballooned to 149,985. Many agents were hunting down possible accomplices who may have provided money, shelter, or some other support to the hijackers. One reporter noted at the time that "the flow of data is crushing; every day brings new leads—and new dead ends." [57] Even so, agents very soon began to get a chilling picture of the complexity of the terrorist operation of September 11.

Early in the investigation, agents were able to identify the nineteen men who had hijacked the four planes. The hijackers were not from one country; they carried passports from Lebanon, Egypt, Saudi Arabia, and the United Arab Emirates. But while they were not countrymen, the nineteen almost certainly were united in their radical Islamic beliefs and their eagerness to wage a jihad, or holy war, against the United States.

Remarkably, the attacks had taken between three and five years to plan, and some experts in Middle East terrorism estimated that to accomplish what they did, at least one hundred people had to have been involved in some way. One intelligence official confided that the FBI feared that there could be between thirty and fifty teams of terrorists still on the loose. "There's more," he said. "More than we have accounted for." [58]

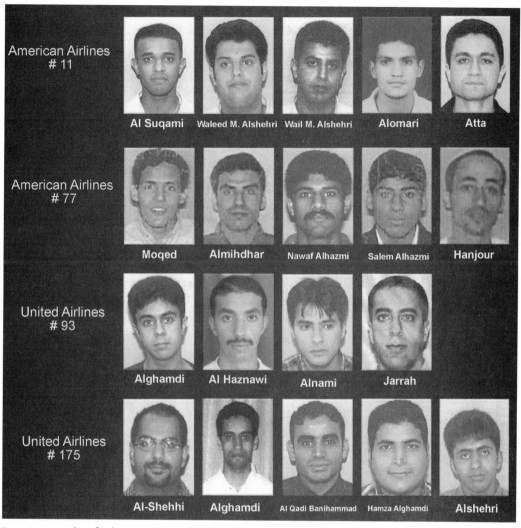

American Airlines
11

Al Suqami   Waleed M. Alshehri   Wail M. Alshehri   Alomari   Atta

American Airlines
77

Moqed   Almihdhar   Nawaf Alhazmi   Salem Alhazmi   Hanjour

United Airlines
93

Alghamdi   Al Haznawi   Alnami   Jarrah

United Airlines
175

Al-Shehhi   Alghamdi   Al Qadi Banihammad   Hamza Alghamdi   Alshehri

Investigators identified nineteen men from several countries who had hijacked the four planes.

Carefully Chosen Planes

As experts pieced together what occurred before the crashes, the extent of the planning became evident. For instance, it was clear that the hijackers, or those directing them, had chosen their planes very carefully. The planes were all westbound transcontinental flights—which meant that they were carry-ing between ten thousand and twenty-four thousand gallons of highly explosive fuel. Experts were in agreement that the intense heat generated by the burning fuel was responsible for the World Trade Center's structural collapse.

The terrorists also chose a Tuesday, almost always the quietest day of the week on such flights, for their operation. This ensured that the hijackers would have fewer passengers to control or subdue. They also chose the particular flights because of when they took off from their respective airports. "To achieve surprise," explains one source, "the attack had to be carefully coordinated so that all four airliners, leaving from three different cities, hit their targets within minutes of each other."[59] Investigators learned, as they went through airline computers, that some of the hijackers traveled on these exact flights for months before September 11—dry runs, most likely, for the actual attack.

As for the weapons used—knives and box cutters—investigators were uncertain whether the hijackers had a source within the airports who could stash the weapons on board beforehand or whether airport security was so lax that the crude weapons did not even register on the walk-through metal detectors before the terrorists boarded their flights. Either scenario, one investigator said, was disturbing.

"Three Hundred Sunny Days a Year"

Even before investigators began digging through the backgrounds of the terrorists, those who were working in air traffic control suspected that the men knew something about airplanes. They had turned off the planes' transponders, which would not have occurred to someone without some knowledge of commercial airplanes.

Two Terrorists Check In

In their Time *magazine article "The New Breed of Terrorist," Johanna McGeary and David Van Biema retrace the check-in of two of the hijackers right before they boarded Flight 77.*

"It was so ordinary at the time, so ominous in hindsight. An American Airlines agent at Dulles Airport in Virginia looked up as two men of Arab origin handed over their tickets. Odd: they were waiting in the coach-class line, dressed in inexpensive clothes, but their tickets were first class, one way. Prepaid at $2,400 each. 'Oil money,' thought the agent. Such passengers are common at Dulles, but these two looked a little bit young: one, around 20, spoke a little English; his brother, even younger, spoke none. And they seemed awfully thin, almost underfed. The agent saw they had ordered special Muslim meals, but so had some others on the flight.

The brothers gave the right answers to standard security questions and had valid IDs, one of them a proper-looking Commonwealth of Massachusetts driver's license. The agent wasn't in a rush and laughed to himself that the two brothers were such infrequent flyers that they didn't know they could check in at the empty first-class counter. But the two were patient, pleasant, low key.

There was really nothing to trigger alarms as the brothers and three other passengers of Arab ethnicity boarded American Airlines Flight #77 for Los Angeles. The two brothers were Nawaq Alhamzi and Salem Alhamzi, who knew they were going to die that morning."

The hijackers attended commercial flight schools where they learned to pilot planes like this one.

But as agents followed the terrorists' trail backwards in an effort to find their associates still at large, they learned that the hijackers had more than a passing interest in flying. In fact, at least one terrorist on each airplane was a certified pilot. And what was most disturbing was that most had attended commercial flight schools in the United States.

Perhaps, say experts, that should not be too surprising, for the United States trains many of the world's pilots. "The backs of international pilot magazines are crammed with ads for flight schools in Florida, California, and Arizona," explains one researcher. "'Three hundred sunny days a year,' some of them proclaim.... If Harvard, Yale and M.I.T. draw the world's future biochemists, these small four- and five-plane aviation schools attract the globe's future pilots."[60]

Air Time

These small U.S. flight schools attract students from around the world for other reasons. Gas and airplane rental is cheap—often about fifty-five dollars per hour, which is about half of what rental would cost at airports near larger cities. What's more, pilot training in other countries is either not available or too costly. As a result of all these factors, commercial flight schools in the United States train about seventy thousand pilots each year.

For instance, the two hijackers who flew the planes that hit the World Trade towers trained at several U.S. flight schools, among them Huffman Aviation, located between Tampa and Fort Myers, Florida. Mohamed Atta, who flew Flight 11, and his cousin Marwan Al-Shehhi, who flew Flight 175, spent thousands of dollars in cash learning to fly small single-engine planes—a must before learning to fly passenger jets.

The two also paid thousands of dollars for time on expensive simulators—often $250 or more per hour. Both Atta and Al-Shehhi were reportedly eager to get beyond small planes and fly jets. Simulators allowed them to experience what flying a three-engine jet was like. Explains one researcher:

Flight simulators gave the hijackers the opportunity to practice techniques for flying passenger jets.

The 727 full-motion simulator is a multimillion-dollar contraption that twists and bucks and turns on hydraulic pistons like a Disney ride. But the technology is good enough that airline pilots use simulators regularly to train for emergencies that are too dangerous to practice in a real plane: a double-engine failure or a fire on takeoff. [61]

After the attacks, people connected with these and other flight schools were both angry and embarrassed. One man said he felt used, because all of his teaching had been twisted into something evil. Another said that looking back, he is surprised he wasn't more suspicious. "It was a little strange that all they wanted to do was turns," says one flight school owner. "Most people who come here want to do takeoffs and landings." [62]

Blending In

Investigators found that many of the terrorists were in the United States for six months or more before the September 11 attacks and that some were in the United States as far back as January 2000. What is alarming to agencies such as the FBI and the Central Intelligence Agency (CIA) is how much they differed from the intelligence community's profile of a typical suicide terrorist—a person who almost certainly would have been noticed early on.

The classic suicide terrorist, based on the profile of others through the years, would be a loner and quite young—between eighteen and twenty-four. He would be fanatic in his actions and his beliefs—a stern, outwardly very moralistic person who would never smoke or use alcohol. In addition, he would be extremely ignorant of many devices of modern technology, and would have neither the ability nor the interest in joining the activities of the larger society.

The nineteen men who committed the suicide attacks on September 11 could not have been further from that profile. They were older—most in their mid- to late twenties, and one was thirty-three. Several were married and had children. When investigators conducted hundreds of interviews with those who had lived or worked near any of the hijackers, almost no one sensed that they were different or suspicious. "My kids played with his kids," says one San Diego neighbor. "I was stunned."[63]

Mastering the Technology

Far from being ignorant of modern technology, the terrorists were technologically very savvy—from the complexities of flying an airplane to video and computer games. Neighbors of some of the terrorists recall that the men spent hours playing computer flight simulator games at night. With a horrible irony, *Time* magazine's Nancy Gibbs notes, "The Microsoft flight simulator and Fly! II—the two most popular simulators for personal computers—allow you to pretend to fly between the World Trade Center towers, and into them. Anyone looking to practice can buy the software off the shelf."[64]

Investigators followed paper trails—receipts, tickets, and other clues—that showed that the hijackers lived in dozens of different cities. They were divided into four small groups, called cells. Each of the cells would eventually be responsible for the hijacking of its particular airplane. The FBI found no evidence that the cells met face-to-face; it is very possible that they never saw one another.

However, it was crucial that the members of each cell communicate with one another, particularly as September 11 neared. Much of this communication was done via the Internet. Agents found hundreds of e-mails on computers in various public libraries. The messages, written in both English and Arabic, openly discussed the hijacking four weeks before it occurred.

"Like Rattling Doors Through the Neighborhood"

What became frustrating to many agents was the way the terrorists were able to do so much damage using freely available technology. Some have compared them to a judo expert who knows the secret of beating a bigger opponent is to use the opponent's strength and size against him. "Bin Laden's operatives," notes one researcher, "have learned how to turn two of America's greatest strengths—openness and technology—into weapons against the American people."[65]

Oregon senator Ron Wyden, a member of the Senate Intelligence Committee, finds that discouraging. "The ability to take our expertise and turn it on us is exhilarating to them," he says. "They stay at it and stay at it to learn how to defeat our technological systems. It's like rattling doors through the neighborhood, looking for one to break in. That's what they're doing with our technology."[66]

The Twentieth Hijacker?

One of the aspects of the case that initially puzzled investigators was the finding that three of the flights had five-man cells, and the fourth—Flight 93, which went down in Pennsylvania—had only four. That led officials to wonder if there had been a twentieth person who did not make the flight for some reason.

That speculation led agents to a thirty-four-year-old man from Morocco who was arrested on immigration charges less than a month before the attacks. Instructors at an Eagan, Minnesota, flight school had become suspicious when the man offered them a great deal of cash if they would teach him how to steer a large plane. He did not, instructors said, want to learn how to land or take off.

After the attacks on September 11, French investigators told U.S. agents that the man had long been on their "watch list" of people suspected of being terrorists. He remained in custody but refused to speak

The New York City skyline is obscured by thick smoke from the attacks on the twin towers.

The Pentagon burns in the distance. The White House (lower left) was evacuated when air traffic controllers thought it was the target.

with investigators. "I don't know what his intentions were for September 11," said a Minnesota official. "But whatever it was, he was unable to carry them out because he was in custody."[67]

Anger Turned Inward

While following the threads of evidence such as this one in Minnesota began to give investigators a clearer picture of the terrorists, it also supported what many officials in Washington, D.C., had been saying since the September 11 attacks. Agencies such as the CIA, the FBI, and others who are in the business of gathering intelligence and upholding the nation's security had failed mightily. Many in Washington were openly angry at the FBI

and the CIA, saying that what occurred on September 11 was the most massive failure of readiness the nation had ever seen. "After we identify the party or parties who were responsible for this," promised Maine senator Olympia Snowe, "we will also have to identify what went wrong on our side."[68]

No one denies that it was the terrorists and their backers who were responsible for the attacks and the deaths of thousands of people—and it is they who should be the target of U.S. anger. However, it is also true that the United States was caught unprepared—landmarks destroyed, four planes hijacked, and thousands killed by men armed only with box cutters and knives. How could such a thing have happened? Where were the

Waiting and Watching

In the days after the terror-
ist attacks, U.S. intelligence
agencies were feverishly going back over old
tips they had received, wondering how they
could have known which were accurate and
which were false. In this excerpt from his
Newsweek *article "We've Hit the Targets,"*
Michael Hirsch relates why some of the infor-
mation being fed to U.S. intelligence might
have been intentionally leaked by bin Laden's
terrorists.

"Some counterterrorism operatives now speculate that intelligence picked up by U.S. agencies about possible terrorist attacks on Americans last June may actually have been leaked by operatives associated with bin Laden. Now it appears the terrorists 'may have been testing where and how we picked up information—and what were the things

we missed,' says a U.S. investigator based in the Persian Gulf. 'They saw where we react-ed, and presumably also where we didn't react.' Were they casing American airports to see if extra precautions went into effect? 'They not only know how to plan, but they know how to test,' said this source, 'and they know, obviously, where the gaps are.'

Among the worst of those gaps is the ram-shackle state of security checks at U.S. air-ports. The ability of unknown bombers to exploit these soft spots—and to do it so jar-ringly, ripping a hole in the heart of America's financial and military power—could itself have serious consequences. For it demon-strates that it can be done again. In fact, ter-rorism experts say that for years their worst fear has been that a suicide bomber would hit inside U.S. borders."

people who were charged with keeping America safe?

For Americans who always thought of their country as powerful in world affairs, see-ing it so easily attacked was both frightening and humiliating. One twenty-one-year-old marine corporal said that he talked to his fam-ily soon after the attacks to get their reaction. "They felt embarrassed," he admitted. "They thought we had more protection as a coun-try." [69]

While quick to offer their sympathy and support, U.S. allies were appalled at the lack of American readiness. "At least 19 people worked for as long as five years," wrote one journalist in Britain's *Economist*, "mostly in

the United States, on a complex operation to crash multiple airliners into several targets. And America's $30 billion-dollar-a-year intel-ligence services barely got a whiff of them. Why not?" [70]

Denial

Many experts agreed that even though the intelligence community should have known more hard facts, those agencies are not entire-ly to blame. Various parts of government had been given warnings all along, but few officials took those warnings seriously. In early 2001, for instance, the CIA told the Senate Intelligence Committee that Osama bin Laden posed the most immediate threat to the United States and its citizens around the world. But because the United States had not suffered large terrorist attacks in the past, many people—including Congress—assumed it could never happen.

The American military was also guilty of a kind of denial. In 1998 the Pentagon made a detailed assessment of ways in which it might be vulnerable to an attack, and personnel offered ideas about correcting possible weaknesses. According to one official who was involved in the assessment, the military response was simply: "No one would dare attack the Pentagon."[71]

The same sluggishness affected the Federal Aviation Authority (FAA), the government agency that is responsible for air safety in the United States. After an explosion on board TWA Flight 800 in 1996 which killed 230 passengers, a panel of experts was asked to make recommendations to keep the nation's air travel safer and more secure. There was no evidence that terrorism was involved in that tragedy; even so, many of the panel's recommendations for airlines and airports were made with the idea that future terrorism was a grave threat to the nation.

Ignored

One member of the panel is convinced that Congress and others in Washington—including the FAA—disregarded their recommendations for the very reason that Flight 800 was an accident rather than a terrorist attack. There was no threat, and therefore no sense of urgency that made fixing the system a priority. "The FAA returned to business as usual," he says, "the commission's recommendations . . . all but ignored."[72]

But the attacks of September 11 were not accidents, and afterward there seemed to be no lack of urgency among the nation's leaders. Security was a top priority. From examination of other possible terrorist weapons, to plans to increase safety on airplanes, to strategies to put more muscle in the intelligence-gathering agencies, the United States was feverishly looking for ways to make sure that such horrors never happened again.

Chapter Five

Taking Stock

O ne of the results of the attacks on September 11 was that people began thinking more seriously about ways in which they felt vulnerable. Not surprisingly, one of the first areas to receive scrutiny was air travel. After all, the hijackers showed that passenger planes loaded with thousands of gallons of fuel could, in the hands of suicidal pilots, be turned into weapons of mass destruction. With 670 million passengers traveling each year, airline safety was a critical priority.

"The Security of a Laundromat"

Immediately after learning about the hijacked planes—and not knowing whether other hijackings were planned for that day—President Bush ordered all flights grounded. Before air travel could resume, changes were put in place. Experts hoped the new precau-

tions would lessen the threat of terrorists destroying airports or taking over airplanes. Curbside check-in was banned to eliminate the risk of car bombs, and only ticketed passengers would be able to go to the boarding gates. In addition, random identification checks of pilots and crew would be made, to make certain that those controlling the airplanes were who they claimed to be.

Some of these changes were not directly related to the ways the hijackers gained control of the airplanes on September 11. Instead, they would fill in what experts believed were dangerous gaps in airline security. These new policies would make it more difficult for terrorists to take over planes in the future.

Interestingly, none of these precautions were new ideas; experts had been calling for better security measures for more than ten years. One aviation consultant scoffs that American airports "have the security of a Laundromat." And while the events of September 11 horrified him, he was not surprised that such breaches of security occurred on airplanes. "No airport can be made totally secure," he insists. "But [the attacks] show that the FAA's security programs are lethally worthless. The FAA has blood on its hands." [73]

Many aviation experts agree, saying that for years, the airline industry had been receiving warnings from a variety of sources that there were problems that could lead to hijackings, bombings, and other terrorist acts. Just weeks before the attacks, a veteran pilot admitted that security was lax. He told one reporter, "It's absurd to think we're safe." [74]

Before the Plane Takes Off

Many security problems have occurred during passenger check-in at airports. Those going to the gate areas are required to walk through metal detectors while their purses and other carry-ons are x-rayed by a scanner. These devices are operated by airport security personnel, who watch the scanner's screen for items that could be guns, knives, or explosives.

However, breaches at these checkpoints have been all too common. In 1998, FAA agents posing as passengers found that they could carry guns under their belts without guards realizing it. If the alarm on the metal detector sounded, the guards would assume that the passengers' belt buckles had set off the sensor, and they would wave the agents through.

Part of the problem, say aviation consultants, is that the companies who are hired to supply airport security pay very low wages—barely minimum wage. As a result, the level of turnover at security positions is very high. At Boston's Logan Airport, for example, the turnover rate from May 1998 to April 1999 was an astonishing 207 percent for security staff. Not surprisingly, many are inexperienced

Passengers line up to be screened at an airport security checkpoint.

workers, says one writer, "who regularly confess that they can't tell or don't care what the mystery object on the x-ray is."[75]

Since the attacks of September 11, the list of banned carry-ons was lengthened. Because the terrorists were able to take control of the four airplanes with only knives and box cutters, new restrictions prohibited passengers from carrying anything that could cut—plastic or metal knives, razor blades, corkscrews, and even metal nail files.

For security personnel who had not been consistently able even to spot definite taboos such as hunting knives and guns, the new regulations were even more difficult. In fact, just a few days after the attacks, a Northwest Airlines flight crew member walked a knife and a corkscrew through a security checkpoint in the Phoenix, Arizona, airport—just to demonstrate how little security screening of passengers had changed. "Clearly," admitted one airport representative, "we have to make some adjustments to tighten things up. We aren't there yet."[76]

"Maybe That's Not So Bad!"

In addition to armed guards who were put to work after September 11, many of the one

---

A Perfect Record in Airline Safety

If the United States wants a model for an airline security plan that really works, officials should take a look at Israel's. No flight out of Ben Gurion Airport, near Tel Aviv, has ever been hijacked. However, as reporter Lisa Beyer explains in "Is This What We Really Want?" the process is long and unsettling, even for the innocent traveler.

"How do the Israelis do it? For one thing, El Al [the national airline] puts at least one armed, plainclothes sky marshal on all its flights. One such agent foiled a hijack attempt over Holland in 1970. During El Al flights, the cockpit door, made of reinforced steel strong enough to repel fire from a handgun, remains locked.

On the ground, the Israelis not only use the standard metal detectors and x-ray machines but also lean on teams of young agents, dressed in blue slacks and white shirts, who interrogate, to varying degrees, every passenger departing Ben Gurion and, in airports abroad, anyone flying El Al. The questions can include: 'When did you book this flight?' 'Who paid for the ticket?' 'Why are you traveling?' 'Whom did you meet while in Israel?' Business travelers are asked for documents proving they actually are pursuing a particular deal. Journalists are asked to reveal the stories they are going to cover. One agent will ask questions for a while, then a second will ask many of the same. The two will compare notes, and one or the other will ask a third batch of questions. This process often takes 20 minutes; it can take two hours.

The idea is to turn up inconsistencies in a terrorist's made-up story . . . and also expose individuals who may be unknowing accomplices. In 1986 El Al security at London's Heathrow airport discovered a bomb sewn into the suitcase of an unwitting Irish woman after she revealed that she had had a romance with a Jordanian, who had bought her the bag."

Airports have added more security, like explosives-sniffing dogs, since the September 11 attacks.

hundred large airports in the United States have explosives-sniffing dogs on patrol as well. Airports have also been urged to do more thorough searches of passengers about to board their flights—having guards routinely frisk passengers for weapons that may have been missed by a scanner, for instance.

However, people in the airline industry worry because such extensive searches and scans will take more time. Passengers would be inconvenienced by having to arrive at the airport even earlier so that they can wait in line to be searched and questioned. Some

wondered if Americans—used to many freedoms—would resent not only the delays but also the invasive nature of such searches. "It's like someone looking through your shopping bags when you're leaving a store, making sure you didn't shoplift," says one woman. "I think that's invasive. It's really treating everyone as a criminal. I know people might put up with it for a month or so at the airports, but I don't think people will be patient for long."[77]

But many passengers say they feel far more secure with the extra precautions. They do not mind waiting in line, because they feel that the airlines are looking out for their safety. "I don't care about frisking and baggage checks and my so-called rights being potentially violated," one business executive maintains. "You go to some places and see guys in flak jackets holding machine guns, and you think, 'Whoa, this is scary.' Now you think, 'Whoa, maybe that's not so bad!'" [78]

Too Many People

Another potential security problem is the number of people in and around the airplane before it takes off. Luggage handlers, mechanics, cleaners, fuelers, and food service personnel all have access to each plane. By law, all of these individuals are supposed to have had background checks, but because of the time and effort required by their various employers, only a small fraction of the people have actually been checked.

This can be as much of a problem, say experts, as a passenger with a weapon. "It's pointless," says one researcher, "to keep a terrorist from carrying aboard a gun if the catering-truck driver can stow one among the beef stews." [79]

But keeping a plane on the tarmac secure has been a difficult task, and one that security experts have been warning airports about for years. In 1999, for example, the Department of Transportation conducted field tests at some of the nation's largest airports and discovered a number of major security problems that were particularly disturbing.

Airport security personnel hand search carry-on luggage. Many passengers feel safer with extra security measures in place.

They sent agents into airports without proper identification and found that they were able to enter off-limits areas in 117 out of 173 tries (a success rate of 68 percent) and were able to board airplanes unchallenged. These agents walked though checkpoints or card-access doors behind unsuspecting airport workers and even drove cars through unguarded gates marked Airplane Personnel Only.

The most critical step, say experts, is a massive effort to comply with laws that already exist, such as criminal background checks on everyone who comes into contact with an airplane. Such checks would encompass not only police databases, but also those on which global intelligence groups post names of suspected terrorists.

In addition, employee identification badges must be updated, so that misplaced or stolen badges will be useless. Some have proposed that U.S. airports should work toward fingerprint-generated security gates, to make it impossible for a terrorist to disguise himself as an airline worker.

Sharing Information

The fact that at least some of the hijackers of September 11 bought tickets under their own names prompted a great amount of criticism—not only for the airlines but also for the FBI, who admitted having some of the names on their "watch list." (The list includes names of people suspected of being involved in terrorist groups that have targeted the United States).

This was more than frustrating for John Michael Loh, a retired air force general. Loh was part of a panel of experts that made strong recommendations to the FAA back in

Better communication between law enforcement agencies might help identify terrorists before they board an airplane.

1996 about keeping the airlines and airports secure. According to Loh, the panel insisted that airline safety be equated with national security. One of their first recommendations was strong communication among agencies such as the FBI, the FAA, and the CIA with airports and airline security.

If investigators share information about potential terrorists with the airlines, airline personnel would know immediately if a person on that list buys a ticket, and airport security could alert the FBI immediately. FBI agents could provide airlines not only with names of suspected terrorists, but also with photographs and possible aliases.

Profiling?

The panel also recommended profiling of passengers—a system of taking into account

A Dilemma

One of the antiterrorism tools likely to be used more often by airline security is profiling—looking more suspiciously at passengers of Middle Eastern ethnicity. In his Star-Tribune *editorial, Matthew Miller relates how fear of flying since September 11 has resulted in his having conflicting feelings about profiling and fairness.*

"On the ground in Minneapolis, after taking our seats, I craned my neck to scrutinize every passenger. I must have looked quite intent, because the flight attendant came right over.

'Can I help you?' she asked. 'What are you looking for?'

I didn't hesitate or hide it. 'I'm looking for Arabs,' I said.

I know it sounds awful, I added defensively, but this is real life. She nodded sympathetically.

'Our security people have been over the manifest three times,' she said. 'We're very comfortable that we're OK.'

I looked in the direction of two 20-something males with dark complexions who appeared to be traveling without families.

'What about them?' I asked.

'They're Mexicans,' she said instantly.

I felt terrible afterward—confused and ashamed, but also determined. All I cared about was that my daughter and I were safe.

In the days since, we've heard many stories about Arabs being taken off flights at the request of fearful flyers and crews. I understand these fears, not least because we see fresh stories daily about airline security—amazingly—still being lax.

Maybe you've experienced my emotional split personality. Part of me feels that if, God forbid, another act of terrorism occurs and Arabs are the perpetrators, the authorities will be more than justified in applying serious new levels of scrutiny to Arabs in the United States. . . . Yet part of me feels heartsick that things could come to this pass. . . . And so I wondered: If more attacks gave our government little choice but to profile aggressively, could there be a way to acknowledge the injustice for the 99.9 percent of the 3.5 million Arab-Americans who might feel humiliated and wronged by it?"

a whole series of variables with the goal of red-flagging someone for closer scrutiny by investigators. One security expert says by collecting and storing more information about people purchasing airline tickets, airlines can avoid more terrorist attacks. "You could then look at a passenger manifest," he explains, "and see that you have a high number of Middle Eastern Muslims. With flight training. Who very rarely fly. You'd see this is anomalous. You wouldn't pull them off, but you'd put an extra marshal onboard."[80]

But many object to the invasion of privacy that such information gathering involves. They say, too, that civil liberties will be curtailed—that certain groups will be targeted simply because of their religion or ethnic background. Says one Stanford University scholar, "I think it would be a tragic irony if [in the name of security] we gave up the very freedoms we are trying to protect as a nation. It would be the ultimate victory for terrorists if they succeed in transforming our society from free and open to closed and paranoid."[81]

"Wrestle Him to the Floor and Keep Him There"

But what if a terrorist is able to fool the security guards and machines and ticket takers' computers, and gets on an airplane? Measures are already being taken so that even a suicidal terrorist would be unable to turn an airplane into a guided missile. One immediate change is the addition of extra sky marshals—armed law enforcement officers. Sky marshals, dressed in plain clothes, have been used on random flights for decades, but far more are now needed than the thirty-eight or forty that had been on the job before September 11.

It is clear, too, that it was far too easy for terrorists to gain access to the controls of the planes, so airlines began working on reinforcing cockpit doors of airplanes. Using deadbolts and Kevlar, the material used to make bullet-proof vests, airlines will make the cockpit doors virtually impenetrable.

Perhaps the most practical source of security on airplanes are the passengers themselves. The heroism that was demonstrated by several passengers on Flight 93 provided a model that many officials admit could make terrorism far less of a threat. A pilot on a flight from Washington, D.C. to Denver just a few days after the attacks reminded passengers that there were some things they themselves could do if someone among them threatened to hijack the plane:

Every one of you should stand up and immediately throw things at the person—pillows, books, magazines, eyeglasses, shoes, anything that will throw him off balance. Most important: get a blanket over him, then wrestle him to the floor and keep him there. We'll land the plane at the nearest airport, and the authorities will take it from there. Remember, . . . there will be one of him and maybe a few confederates, but there are 200 of you. You can overwhelm them.[82]

What If?

But while keeping air travel secure is a high priority, it is not the only aspect of terrorism that raises concerns. Even before the attacks of September 11, defense officials, medical experts, and others had worked out a list of "what ifs." What if terrorists had weapons of mass destruction, such as a nuclear device? What if terrorists used chemical or biological weapons? What if they gained access to a city's water supply or a food plant?

While the thought of one of these events occurring is frightening, considering such scenarios is important. For government officials trying to prevent terrorists from harming Americans, such hard questions point out ways in which the United States is vulnerable. "A central tenet of counterterrorism," explains one researcher, "is that, to defend yourself, you must identify the targets that need defending."[83]

One security worry has to do with the intentional spread of a dangerous disease or chemical. In 1995 a Japanese terrorist cult released sarin, an odorless, colorless gas that affects the nervous system, on a subway platform in Tokyo. Twelve people died by breathing the gas, although the death toll could have been much higher. The idea that such a substance could be so easily and anonymously set off in a crowd was frightening to many people.

However, chemical weapons are expensive to produce—especially in the large amounts needed to kill a lot of people. Says one chemical weapons expert, "Any bozo can make a chemical agent in a beaker, but producing tons and tons is difficult."[84] More of a concern, say terrorism strategists, is germ warfare—the introduction of disease into a population.

Bioterrorism

Disease control experts say that there are several possibilities, but the two most likely to be used by terrorists would be smallpox and anthrax. Smallpox, a virus that had been eradicated from developed countries before the 1970s, is highly contagious, and experts say it could spread through a large city in a few days, killing tens of thousands. Because smallpox has not been seen in the United States for decades, very few people today are immunized. An outbreak would be deadly, say doctors, because there is not enough of the vaccine currently available to protect every American.

Anthrax, though not contagious, is a disease caused by bacteria, and when inhaled, kills 90 percent of its victims. Just weeks after the attacks on the Pentagon and World Trade

Center, cases of anthrax began showing up—first in Florida, then in New York, Washington, New Jersey, and Connecticut. Anonymous letters containing spores of the germ arrived in a number of locations—from the mail room of a tabloid publisher to the offices of a U.S. senator, a network news anchor, and that of a hospital worker. Some postal employees and others who touched the letters got skin anthrax, an easily treatable form of the dis-

This envelope and letter mailed to Senator Tom Daschle contained anthrax.

ease. However, others inadvertently inhaled the dustlike spores and were infected with a more deadly form of anthrax, which proved fatal.

As of March 2002, no one could say with certainty who was responsible for the spread of the anthrax germs—or even if the instances of anthrax were related to the September 11 tragedy. However, it was clear that the germ had been weaponized—that is, *some* person or group had changed the anthrax spores into a form that would be more likely to infect people.

Doctors called for increased production of antibiotics that would treat anthrax, and post offices in targeted areas began using irradiation machinery to kill any spores in the mail. The machines, said Postmaster General John Potter, would cost about $2.5 billion. "This new technology is not cheap," he admitted, "but we are committed to spending what it takes to make the mail safe." [85]

What Are the Targets?

An important part of national security after September 11 was to take another look at public places that might be targets for future terrorist attacks. Anywhere in which thousands of people would gather at one time was a possibility, and there were many.

Once both major league baseball and the National Football League had resumed their schedules after approximately a week's delay, fans returned to a slightly different type of stadium. More security personnel were checking purses and backpacks as people entered. Some stadiums had already installed metal detectors at the gates. Airplanes were not permitted to fly overhead, at least temporarily; any aircraft violating the rule would be intercepted or shot down by patrolling air force jets.

Many outdoor theme parks, such as Disneyland and Sea World, stepped up security in a similar fashion. Security staff paid more attention to camera cases, diaper bags, and other carrying cases, and additional uniformed police were on patrol. Because the many families who visit such parks are so spread out—more, say, than spectators in a stadium are—experts say that an attack in these places would have little chance of hurting great numbers of people.

Dangerous Skyscrapers

Even if airplanes are not used to topple skyscrapers, such buildings could still be likely targets for a terrorist attack. Since 1995 when the federal building in Oklahoma City was destroyed by a truck packed with explosives, many buildings around the United States installed concrete barricades to keep vehicles away. However, such barricades are not an option for many buildings because of their location in crowded downtown areas.

For those buildings, engineers recommend replacing glass windows with laminated glass. The latter is less apt to splinter in a bomb explosion than regular glass. In addition, many of the newest tall buildings are being built with tiny sensors embedded in the concrete frames, which would trigger an alarm if the building's beams were so seriously damaged that the building could collapse. That way, workers and emergency personnel would know they had to evacuate.

Skyscrapers' ventilation systems could be a problem, too. If a terrorist released anthrax or a virus such as smallpox into a vent, it could circulate throughout the building. However, filters equipped with special devices that can disinfect the air with ultraviolet light have been developed. These filters can screen out most toxins, including anthrax and smallpox. Engineers say it is a good idea for any building maintenance staff to make sure their ventilation systems are secure and up-to-date.

Cyber-Terrorism

Viruses of another sort are a concern to terrorism experts, too—those that can destroy a computer's hard drive. Such viruses are not merely an inconvenience, for critically important systems run on computer networks: telephone networks, airport security, the 911 system, and the banking system, to name just a few.

Most of these systems and networks have installed various forms of protection against such attacks, making it difficult for a computer terrorist to hack into a system of such importance. However, conducting its own tests in 1997, the National Security Agency had some of its best agents try to get into such systems, with worrisome results. Without being specific about which programs the agents were able to break into, one Pentagon spokesman admitted, "We learned that hackers could have a dramatic impact on the nation's infrastructure, including the power grid [the network of power plants throughout the eastern part of the United States and Canada]." [86]

Since that time, much has been done to safeguard those systems. The concerns that

Skyscrapers such as the Sears Tower in Chicago, Illinois, are likely targets of a terrorist attack.

Y2K would result in massive computer problems turned out to be a positive thing, for it forced experts to carefully examine computer networks and the protections they require. Even so, the attacks of September 11 made many computer technicians uneasy. Says one computer security researcher, "Since September 11, I can confirm that there's been a lot of action to make sure [key routes on the networks] are properly maintained." [87]

"I Just Want It All to Go Away"

As the recovery work at Ground Zero, at the Pentagon, and that of the medical examiners attempting to identify remains of the dead continued after the attacks, the nation was forced to move on. Critical aftershocks of the attacks, such as the war against terrorists in Afghanistan and the mounting anxiety over the spread of anthrax, occupied much of the government's attention. Various agencies and departments at national, state, and local levels were hard at work—either in preventing future threats or in dealing with crises resulting from the attacks of September 11.

While government departments and agencies were involved in those crucial jobs, the American people were facing different sorts of crises on a more personal level. "It's like there's the 'me' at work, and the 'me' the minute I walk out of the hospital," says Mickey, an emergency medical worker who has been taking a crash course on dealing with a smallpox outbreak. "When I'm at work, I'm dealing with stuff that might happen, and I feel like, okay, I'm contributing a little bit.

"But then, I leave, I get in my car, and I feel like a different person. I'm nervous, I'm edgy, I don't know. I know a lot of guys that are like me—it's the way we feel since September 11. I'm walking around in a fog. I think if I had a wish, I'd wish we could go back to September 10 and catch these guys before they got on their damned planes. I just want it all to go away; I want everything to be normal again." [88]

But as many Americans struggled with a range of emotions that they had not felt before, the hope of getting their lives back to normal in the weeks afterward seemed more impossible every day. Perhaps, as some suggested, the events of September 11 were life-changing—not just for the victims and their families, but for all Americans.

Chapter Six

"A New Kind of Life"

Within days after the attacks, government officials urged the American people to resume their lives, to get back to doing the things they always did. If they stayed home or curtailed their normal activities, people were told, the terrorists would have succeeded. So outwardly, the signs of normal life returned. Children went off to school, parents went to work, and television networks began running programs other than news. But a closer look would reveal that life was far from normal.

"I Worry About Everything"

"I'll tell you one change," confides Pam, a coffee shop waitress. "I think a lot of people are like me—suffering from lack of sleep. Right after September 11, I was terrified all the time. I kept hearing airplanes, and I was worried they were going to fly into our apart-

ment building. And that's nuts, because I live in a two-story building, and in *Michigan*, for Pete's sake! I know Osama bin Laden's not targeting me, but I can't help worrying. I worry about everything, and I never used to." [89]

Marnie agrees. She says that she can't get the image of the second airplane hitting the World Trade Center out of her mind—and it's made her more fragile emotionally. "I feel like I'm crying constantly," she says. "I close my eyes and see that image, and it's the most frightening thing I can imagine.

"I think of those people in the building and on the planes, and what they went through," she continues. "I don't want to keep feeling this way, because it isn't helping anyone. And I'm not a weepy sort of person. But I can't move on. I feel like I'm stuck in September 11." [90]

"I Called Him 8,000 Times"

Many people say that as a result of the attacks, they are nervous about being separated from family members, even for a short time. One Chicago woman whose husband works in the Sears Tower says that she fears for his safety at work. She insists that he keep his cell phone on all the time, and she admits that she calls him frequently. One day not long after September 11, she says, "I called him 8,000 times."[91]

Earl, a father of two daughters in college, says that he and his wife got in their car the weekend after the attacks and drove twelve hundred miles "just to be near them. I can't tell you how much better we felt. My wife and I were basket cases before that, just worried sick. But going to see them really helped. I mean, just hugging your kids, telling them how much you love them. I know we felt so much more grounded—we stayed a day and a half, and turned around and drove home! One of my [law] partners said, 'Don't they have telephones at that school?' I said, 'Yeah, but they weren't enough. Telephones just weren't enough.'"[92]

Many people, especially those who live far from New York or Washington, D.C., say they feel foolish worrying about terrorists—especially when people around them seem

While Americans attempt to resume normal lives, many continue to struggle with anxiety, fear, and grief.

calm and unafraid. However, almost all Americans seem to be fighting their own private battles with fear and anxiety. Writes one observer, "Even people who appear to be calm will privately confess: I won't go to the mall anymore. I ask for a low floor at the hotel, near a staircase. I throw up every morning before I get on the train. I thought I heard a crop duster in the middle of the night."[93]

Too Much Coverage?

Many experts believe that the media unwittingly fueled the fears. In the first days after the attacks, all network programming shifted to news about the aftermath, about the new war, and about where the next terrorism would strike. And after regular programming resumed, many people felt the need to keep tuned in to CNN or CNBC.

"I was hooked," says one man. "It was like—okay, I really don't want to know what's happening if it's bad, because I know I'll just be more depressed, but I couldn't really relax unless I turned it on for a few minutes, just to check stuff out. It was like my security blanket, I guess."[94]

But while the constant stream of news and commentary might have been helpful to many people, some found that it fueled their anxieties. One New Yorker agrees. "My wife, she's homebound," he explains. "She reached the point last week where she couldn't watch

Events of September 11 were broadcast on all the networks for days following the attacks and people watched on televisions everywhere.

the news, so I went to Blockbuster's. The place was mobbed. I looked around and everybody was sobbing. They all wanted to get away from it. It was mental overload."[95]

A family therapist in Minneapolis says she advised several of her clients to turn off the television. "I had some who were riveted, maybe watching seven or eight hours a day or more," she says. "It's too much for any of us. I don't think it's healthy or necessary. Better to do something positive or active—go outside, rake some leaves, go for a run or something."[96]

Protection

The heightened anxiety prompted some Americans to prepare for the worst. Around the nation, many army surplus stores reported high demand for gas masks. Those who wanted masks were concerned about another attack, which they feared might be a chemical or biological agent released into the air.

However, while they understood the public's fears, many scientists thought gas masks were a waste of money. "I believe individuals buying gas masks to protect themselves against an unspecified biological or chemical attack is pretty useless," says Dr. John Clements, professor of immunology at Tulane University. Clements says that most toxins would be released quietly into a populated area. In the case of anthrax, for instance, people would not be aware they had been exposed until much later.

"The [anthrax] infection takes one to six days to start showing symptoms," he says. "And you are not going to be aware that you were exposed for some time."[97] In addition,

he adds, many chemical and biological agents are harmful not only from inhalation, but also from being absorbed through the skin; a gas mask would offer no protection for the latter instance.

The Ugly Side of Fear

But while fear made many Americans more depressed and reclusive, fear brought on by the events of September 11 had an aggressive side, too. Angry and wanting to strike back, some struck out against innocent people. In many cities around the United States, there were instances of verbal or physical abuse of people who were—or looked like—Middle Eastern Muslims.

In Mesa, Arizona, a service station owner was shot three times by a passing motorist on September 15, four days after the terrorist attacks. The victim was Hindu, not Muslim. The man police arrested for the crime explained it by saying, "I'm an American."[98]

In New York City, someone threw large rocks through the windshields of taxis in Central Park, apparently targeting only cabs driven by Arabs. Law enforcement agencies nationwide were reporting hate crimes against Muslims and Middle Easterners.

President Bush spoke out against such crimes during his visit to a Washington, D.C., mosque and again before Congress. "We respect your faith," he said. "Its teachings are good and peaceful."[99] He urged Americans to refrain from directing hostility toward Muslims or any other innocent people. But many Muslims who had never faced such hatred in the United States felt suddenly that they were no longer welcome.

Farooq Muhammad (center), a New York City emergency medical technician, is an American and a Muslim. He treated the injured at Ground Zero.

"This Is My Home"

One Muslim who experienced this is Farooq Muhammad, a twenty-six-year-old emergency medical technician in the New York City Fire Department. Born in the United States, his parents came from Pakistan in the 1970s, seeking a better life. After the attack on the World Trade Center, Muhammad went on volunteer duty, helping to treat many victims on the scene.

While he was bandaging the wounded at Ground Zero on September 11, Muhammad says that he became aware of people looking at him, and at his Islamic name on the FDNY polo shirt he was wearing. "I felt ashamed," he says. However, he knows that his religion is not to blame for the acts of the terrorists.

"Looking back, I feel ashamed for feeling ashamed.... Muslims aren't like this. They're peaceful people."[100]

Gus Karim believes that, too. He says, "The Koran says, if a man kills an innocent person, to God it looks like he is killing all innocent people on earth." Karim understands that there will be some who will act without thinking; his own daughter was taunted soon after the attacks. However, he also knows that most Americans would never do such things. A tailor, who is proud to have made the suit President Bush wore for his presidential inauguration, Karim says, "This is my home, and I am proud to be here. I will never forget what this country gave me.... And I want my country to come back together."[101]

Mohammed Ayesh has been the target of anger by some New Yorkers, but like Karim, he tries to understand. "I don't blame them," he says. "Every human being falls into the same thing. They might have had relatives in the towers." Even so, he says, he wants people to realize that Muslims grieved on September 11 like other Americans. "Maybe I don't look like a white boy," he says, "but this tragedy hurt me, too." [102]

"It's Hard Not to Feel Emotional"

However, not all of the changes that came about because of the attacks were negative ones. Many people say they had never felt more proud of being an American after September 11. The American flag became a hot commodity. So many were sold that stores quickly ran out. "We usually sell a lot around the Fourth of July," says one shop owner, "and we kind of take our time reordering. We've

---

Redefining Pop Culture

The dramatic shift in priorities that came about after the terrorist attacks had a profound and immediate effect on the U.S. entertainment industry. In "What's Entertainment Now?" James Poniewozik describes the shift in America's priorities after September 11.

"This, in a way, is the problem facing American pop culture in the wake of the attacks on the World Trade Center and the Pentagon: so much that we could say casually a month ago rings empty, even cruel, today. Our metaphors have expired. Pleasure seems mocking and futile.... Entertainers in every field are in a crisis of relevance, caught up in a nationwide feeling of survivor's guilt, unsure whether their work has any place in the new reality. 'I don't know if my writing right now is adequate to the time,' says playwright Jon Robin Baitz. 'I'm not going to write until I feel that's no longer an issue.'...

'No humor column today,' wrote syndicated funnyman Dave Barry. 'I don't want to write it, and you don't want to read it.' Sports went on hiatus, and after they returned, a preseason hockey game between longtime rivals New York Rangers and Philadelphia Flyers ended with the players watching President Bush's address to Congress, shaking hands and skating off the ice in midgame.... A five-hour Law & Order mini-series was scuttled because it involved an anthrax-attack plot in New York City.... Terror-themed movies were shelved by studios and pulled from cable....

Mainly, pop culture redefined itself in terms of what it now is not. It is not too flippant. David Letterman held the hand of a weeping Dan Rather on a moving return to the air; *The Daily Show's* Jon Stewart tearfully invoked Dr. Martin Luther King Jr....

Above all, it is not too violent. Before September 11, panicked citizens running down a street from a collapsing building was an action-movie cliche.... 'It's going to be a very long time' [predicted one producer] before audiences will watch a building blow up."

never had a rush on flags like this—I've had more than a hundred calls today already from people wanting a flag." [103]

Companies that make flags confirmed the huge demand. In the ten days after the attack, one company in Florida sold more than one hundred thousand flags—a number unheard of in the company's history. Says the owner, "I've got orders on my desk I couldn't fill in a million years." [104]

The women who sew the flags say that they feel that their job is more important since the attacks. "You touch these flags, it's hard not to feel emotional," says one worker. "You know that everybody in the nation is pulling together, that somebody out there really wants this flag. And we need to get it to them." [105] Workers in one Pennsylvania company were very emotional about an order of five hundred flags that would be draped over the caskets of firefighters and other emergency workers who died at the scene of the attacks. At the Florida company, the workers are almost all immigrants. One Cuban-born woman notices that many Americans are for the first time seeing their flag as she and her family saw it twelve years before. They were on a boat with a broken compass, she says, and after three days they were rescued by a U.S. Coast Guard patrol. "The first thing I saw as they pulled their boat up was the American flag," she explains. "That flag meant everything in the world to us. It was the most beautiful thing I had ever seen." [106]

"I Can't Believe This Is Me"

Patriotism showed itself in a number of ways—many of them quite new for some Americans. Some who stood in line to buy flags admitted they had never even considered buying a flag before September 11. "I'll tell you something," says one woman. "I'm a child of the sixties—marching against the war in Vietnam, sit-ins at the Capitol, everything. I used to equate flags with the conservatives, with the politicians. But boy, all that's changed. I've got flags on our house, a flag on the car. I can't believe this is me!" [107]

Others who contend they never felt anything remotely patriotic now are moved to tears by the national anthem sung before a

Stores around the United States sold out of American flags as people began to display them everywhere.

America's New Heroes

Emergency workers—especially firefighters—were visibly heroic on September 11, and the staggering number of deaths in their ranks made the New York City Fire Department a legion of American heroes. The following excerpt is an interview reporter Tom Downey did with firefighter Lincoln Quappe; it appears in the New York Times Magazine. *The interview was done in March 2001; Quappe was listed as missing after the towers collapsed.*

"The rescue companies are the eyes and ears for everyone. If you get a report of people trapped, then we'll spearhead our attack up to that particular area. And maybe be able to control the fire enough to warn the guy upstairs that it's really getting bad here, and maybe it's time for them to get out. At Rescue Two, our main duty is looking out for the safety of all the firemen. Really, that's what we're there for. And we've shown time and again that when there's a fireman hurt, we'll drop everything and get him.

Being a fireman's fireman comes with experience. I still have so much to learn. I only have 16 years on the job. At Rescue Two, I feel like a probie all over again. I found that some of the most unassuming guys are the most fantastic firemen. They're always there at the right time, they're always in position, and in the heat of battle, they never shy away....

When you're in a fire, things are running through your brain a million times a minute. . . . Every fire is scary. That's the way it is. You're a damned liar if you say you're not scared. It's hard to say which fires are the most dangerous. Each is completely different.... Even a silly little fire can get a guy killed. It all comes down to fate. But there are signs that you can pick up on at a fire when it's getting bad. I don't have all the answers, but I have an idea when it's time to go.... I'll be in contact with my guys.... If Bobby says it's time to get out, I'm going. I use him as my guardian angel, because I know he's seen a lot of things in the past. The captain, too. If the captain says, 'We're getting out of here,' I'm going. I don't want to die here."

baseball game. One sixth grader says that his mother taught him and his brothers three verses of "America the Beautiful." "She couldn't believe we never learned it in school," he shrugs. "So we all had to stand there and memorize it before we were allowed to go out. She told us it was important." [108]

Such patriotism is even evident on college campuses. At a University of Michigan football game on September 22, writes one observer, the stadium's emotional reaction to a halftime show surprised the marching band:

In a somber, patriotic tribute, the band formed an American eagle on the field while they played "America the Beautiful." They unfurled a giant flag on the 50-yard line. As she stood saluting, drum major Karen England was stunned by the crowd's reaction. Normally, Michigan football fans clog the aisles at halftime, racing for the concession stands and the restrooms. Instead, the crowd stood as one and sang. After they exited the field to a simple military drum tap, England had to comfort her sobbing bandmates. "I don't think anybody in the band realized the effect this would have," she said. [109]

Shifting Priorities

For some young men and women, the feelings of patriotism have inspired them to enlist either in the armed services or in a service program that would benefit the United States in other ways. A twenty-year-old says that his decision to enlist in the navy has given him a pride in himself that he has not experienced before. One twenty-two-year-old graduate of Emory University was so moved after a trip to Ground Zero that she enlisted in the national service project called AmeriCorps. "I wanted to do more than give blood," she says. "This is something lasting that I can put my energy into." [110]

Many colleges are seeing the shift in students' thinking about their futures, too. Students are requesting classes and seminars to learn Middle Eastern languages, to understand the Islamic religion and the cultures in which it is a key component, and to explore terrorism and its history. Many schools have been more than willing to adjust their curriculum. Says one official at UCLA, "We agreed that it was important to connect the event with what we do here every day—which is teach and learn." [111]

One graduate student says that young people his age have always been known as the generation that had it easy. "We had no crisis, no Vietnam, no Martin Luther King, no JFK," he

says. "We've got it now. When we have kids and grandkids, we'll tell them that we lived through the roaring '90's, when all we cared about was the number one movie or how many copies an album sold. This is where it changes." [112]

The same could be said for the entire nation. The attacks of September 11, 2001, left few Americans unaffected in some way—whether by grief for the thousands of people who died, or by the stories of incredible heroism, the investigations, the economic upheaval, the sudden burst of patriotism, or the declared war. Experts say that it is impossible to say what lasting changes will occur because of the attacks. Certainly vast changes will be made in the way the United States deals with the nations of the Middle East and with the more than 475 million people who come across U.S. borders each year. National security will probably never again be taken for granted, and the departments and agencies that oversee it will be far more vigilant.

"I Just Wanted to See What a 'Normal' Paper Looked Like"

Many Americans feel that they will become more informed as a result of the attacks. "A few days after this happened, I took out a newspaper from September 10," says one college senior. "It was bizarre in a way—like seeing an old shot of the World Trade towers in a movie or something. I just wanted to see what a 'normal' paper looked like, before all the stories had to do with terrorism.

"But I was struck by how little of that paper I'd read! I must have just looked at the

For weeks following September 11, the terrorist attacks were front-page news.

main headlines [and] the sports. I didn't read any of the stories about the Middle East, or Afghanistan, or anything. And there were stories in there. They just didn't seem like they were that relevant to my life. I know a lot of things about me are going to get back to normal. But I hope I'll never go back to being that narrow. I bet a lot of other people feel that way, too."[113]

A Defining Moment

Over time, much of the evidence of the September 11 attacks will be gone. The Pentagon will be repaired. The digging and stabilizing of Ground Zero will eventually be completed, too. The sounds of bulldozers and dump trucks—a constant presence in lower Manhattan since the attacks—will be stilled.

For the American people, the raw feelings of disbelief and fear will fade over time. But the fiery images of airplanes exploding into buildings will remain. The attacks that occurred on that Tuesday morning—September 11, 2001—put an abrupt end to Americans' belief that their country was immune to the kind of violence that plagues the rest of the world.

"Whatever the outcome," wrote one observer just a few days afterward, "it was clear that some things had changed forever. The attacks will become a defining reference point for our culture and imagination, a question of before and after, safe and scarred."[114]

Notes

Introduction: "The Worst of What Humanity Can Do"

1. Clare Arthur, interview by author, Minneapolis, MN, September 21, 2001.
2. Nancy Gibbs, "If You Want to Humble an Empire," *Time* (special edition), n.d., n.p.
3. Quoted in NBC coverage, September 12, 2001.
4. Quoted in "Lending a Hand," *People Weekly,* October 1, 2001, p. 44.

Chapter One: "The Mouth of Hell"

5. Quoted in Mark Clayton, "Controllers' Tale of Flight 11," *Christian Science Monitor,* September 13, 2001, p. 1.
6. Quoted in Clayton, "Controllers' Tale of Flight 11," p. 1.
7. Quoted in Karen Breslau, "Courage in the Air," *Newsweek Commemorative Issue: The Spirit of America,* n.d., p. 33.
8. Adam Gopnik, "The City and the Pillars," *New Yorker,* September 24, 2001, p. 36.
9. Quoted in Anne Cronin, "A Black Cloud. A Shower of Glass. A Glimpse of Hell. Run!" *New York Times,* September 16, 2001, p. 1.
10. Quoted in CNN coverage, September 11, 2001.
11. Quoted in "Comment: Tuesday, and After," *New Yorker,* September 24, 2001, p. 27.
12. "From Our Correspondents," *New Yorker,* September 24, 2001, p. 55.
13. Quoted in Jerry Adler, "Connecting in New York," *Newsweek Commemorative Issue: The Spirit of America,* n.d., p. 24.

14. Quoted in Jim Lynch, ed., *The Day That Changed America* (American Media Publications special edition), n.d., p. 25.
15. Quoted in "From Our Correspondents," p. 55.
16. Quoted in Lynch, *The Day That Changed America,* p. 12.
17. Quoted in Amanda Ripley, "The Last Phone Call," *Time,* September 24, 2001, p. 73.
18. Quoted in Ripley, "The Last Phone Call," p. 75.
19. Quoted in Gibbs, "If You Want to Humble an Empire," n.p.
20. Quoted in "Comment: Tuesday, and After," p. 28.
21. Quoted in "Hell on Earth," *People Weekly,* September 24, 2001, p. 39.
22. Quoted in CBS coverage, September 14, 2001.
23. Quoted in "I Saw Things No One Should Ever See," *Newsweek* (extra edition), n.d., n.p.

Chapter Two: Two New Targets

24. Marc Fisher and Don Phillips, "On Flight 77: 'Our Plane Is Being Hijacked,'" *Washington Post,* September 12, 2001, p. 1A.
25. Sharon Begley, "The Rescue at the Pentagon," *Newsweek Commemorative Issue: The Spirit of America,* n.d., p. 36.
26. Quoted in Stephen Barr, "At the Pentagon: 'All of a Sudden . . . Anything But Routine,'" *Washington Post,* September 12, 2001, p. 2B.
27. Quoted in Begley, "Rescue at the Pentagon," p. 36.

28. Quoted in "Crisis Management," *People Weekly*, September 24, 2001, p. 63.

29. Quoted in Mary Beth Sheridan, "Loud Boom—Then Flames in Hallway," *Washington Post*, September 12, 2001, p. 15A.

30. Begley, "Rescue at the Pentagon," p. 38.

31. Quoted in Barr, "At the Pentagon," p. 2B.

32. Quoted in Jodi Wilgoren and Edward Wong, "On Doomed Flight, Passengers Vow to Perish Fighting," *New York Times*, September 13, 2001, p. 1A.

33. Quoted in Ricardo-Alonso Zaldivar, "After the Attack, Fateful Delay," *Los Angeles Times*, September 20, 2001, p. 9A.

34. Quoted in Josh Tyrangiel, "Facing the End," *Time*, September 24, 2001, p. 68.

35. Quoted in Wilgoren and Wong, "On Doomed Flight," p. 1A.

36. Quoted in Breslau, "Courage in the Air," p. 34.

37. Quoted in Breslau, "Courage in the Air," p. 34.

Chapter Three: A Nation Reacts

38. Quoted in Gibbs, "If You Want to Humble an Empire," n.p.

39. CNN coverage, September 11, 2001.

40. Quoted in Maureen Dowd, "A Grave Silence," *New York Times*, September 12, 2001, p. 27A.

41. Quoted in Roger Segelkin, "CU Veterinarian Aids Rescue Dogs at Site of World Trade Center," *Cornell Chronicle*, September 20, 2001. www.news.cornell.edu/Chronicles/9.20.01/WTC-dogs.html.

42. Quoted in Joel Stein, "Digging Out," *Time*, September 24, 2001, p. 62.

43. Quoted in Richard Lenzin Jones, "A Growing Realization of Unspeakable Loss," *New York Times*, September 15, 2001, p. 20A.

44. Quoted in Jones, "A Growing Realization of Unspeakable Loss," p. 20A.

45. Quoted in Gibbs, "If You Want to Humble an Empire," n.p.

46. Quoted in "The Nation's Neighborhood," *Newsweek Commemorative Issue: The Spirit of America*, p. 42.

47. Shelley, telephone interview by author, September 30, 2001.

48. Quoted in Nancy Gibbs, "Life on the Homefront," *Time*, October 1, 2001, p. 17.

49. Quoted in Gibbs, "Life on the Homefront," p. 17.

50. Quoted in "The Nation's Neighborhood," p. 42.

51. Quoted in "Helping Hands," *Newsweek Commemorative Issue: The Spirit of America*, p. 57.

52. Pam, interview by author, Minneapolis, MN, October 24, 2001.

53. Sue, telephone interview by author, September 29, 2001.

Chapter Four: Looking for Answers

54. Gibbs, "If You Want to Humble an Empire," n.p.

55. Quoted in Lisa Beyer, "The Most Wanted Man in the World," *Time*, September 24, 2001, p. 58.

56. Quoted in Evan Thomas, "A New Day of Infamy," *Newsweek* (extra edition), p. 25.

57. John Cloud, "The Plot Comes into Focus," *Time*, October 1, 2001, p. 51.

58. Quoted in Johanna McGeary and David Van Biema, "The New Breed of Terrorist," *Time*, September 24, 2001, p. 30.

59. Thomas, "A New Day of Infamy," p. 26.

60. McGeary and Van Biema, "New Breed of Terrorist," p. 31.

61. McGeary and Van Biema, "New Breed of Terrorist," p. 32.

62. Quoted in Evan Thomas and Mark Hosenball, "Bush: 'We're at War,'" *Newsweek*, September 24, 2001, p. 32.
63. Quoted in McGeary and Van Biema, "New Breed of Terrorist," p. 32.
64. Gibbs, "If You Want to Humble an Empire," n.p.
65. Quoted in Thomas and Hosenball, "Bush," p. 30.
66. Quoted in Thomas and Hosenball, "Bush," p. 30.
67. Quoted in Pat Doyle, "Under Suspicion: On Terror's Trail in Minnesota," *Star Tribune*, October 7, 2001, p. 1A.
68. Quoted in Terence Samuel, "Plenty of Blame to Go Around," *U.S. News & World Report*, October 1, 2001, p. 28.
69. Quoted in Roger Simon, "A Test of Will," *U.S. News & World Report*, October 1, 2001, p. 12.
70. "United States: Testing Intelligence, National Security," *Economist*, October 6, 2001, p. 31.
71. Quoted in Samuel, "Plenty of Blame to Go Around," p. 28.
72. John Michael Loh and Gerald Kauver, "FAA: A Failure on Aviation Security," *Aviation Week & Space Technology*, October 8, 2001, p. 94.

Chapter Five: Taking Stock

73. Quoted in Sharon Begley, "Will We Ever Be Safe Again?" *Newsweek*, September 24, 2001, p. 58.
74. Quoted in Daniel Eisenberg, "How Safe Can We Get?" *Time*, September 24, 2001, p. 85.
75. Begley, "Will We Ever Be Safe Again?" p. 60.
76. CNN coverage, September 14, 2001.
77. Charleen, telephone interview by author, September 29, 2001.
78. Quoted in Begley, "Will We Ever Feel Safe Again?" p. 61.
79. Begley, "Will We Ever Feel Safe Again?" p. 58.
80. Quoted in Begley, "Will We Ever Feel Safe Again?" p. 60.
81. Quoted in Begley, "Will We Ever Feel Safe Again?" p. 60.
82. Quoted in Gibbs, "Life on the Homefront," p. 17.
83. Sharon Begley, "Procecting America: The Top Ten Priorities," *Newsweek*, November 5, 2001, p. 29.
84. Quoted in Michael Lemonick, "The Next Threat?" *Time*, October 1, 2001, p. 70.
85. Quoted in Begley, "Protecting America," p. 30.
86. Quoted in Begley, "Protecting America," p. 38.
87. Quoted in Begley, "Protecting America," p. 38.
88. Mickey, interview by author, St. Paul, MN, October 30, 2001.

Chapter Six: "A New Kind of Life"

89. Pam, telephone interview by author, September 30, 2001.
90. Marnie, interview by author, St. Paul, MN, October 30, 2001.
91. Quoted in Jeffery Kluger, "Attack on the Spirit," *Time*, September 24, 2001, p. 94.
92. Earl, telephone interview by author, October 12, 2001.
93. Nancy Gibbs, "Shadow of Fear," *Time*, October 22, 2001, p. 27.
94. Brad, telephone interview by author, October 13, 2001.
95. Quoted in Jennifer Senior, "The Circles of Loss," *New York Magazine*, October 1, 2001, p. 37.
96. Lynn, telephone interview by author, November 1 and 2, 2001.
97. Quoted in Alexa Pozniak, "The Air We Breathe," ABC News.com, September 27, 2001. abcnews.go.com/sections/living/DailyNews/WTC-gasmasks010926.html.

98. Quoted in David Van Biema, "As American As . . . ," *Time,* October 1, 2001, p. 72.

99. Quoted in Van Biema, "As American As . . . ," p. 73.

100. Quoted in Daniel Eisenberg, "Feeling the Heat from All Sides," *Newsweek Commemorative Issue: The Spirit of America,* p. 59.

101. Quoted in David Van Biema, "One God and One Nation," *Time,* September 24, 2001, p. 39.

102. Quoted in Catherine Saint Louis, "The Looks They Get," *New York Times Magazine,* September 23, 2001, p. 77.

103. Ed, telephone interview by author, November 2, 2001.

104. Quoted in "Lending a Hand," *People Weekly,* October 1, 2001, p. 40.

105. Quoted in Jonathan Alter, "Patriotism: Filling the Demand," *Newsweek Commemorative Issue: The Spirit of America,* p. 84.

106. Quoted in "Lending a Hand," p. 41.

107. Lela, interview by author, Minneapolis, MN, October 2, 2001.

108. Kyle, interview by author, Bloomington, MN, October 30, 2001.

109. Barbara Kantrowitz and Keith Naughton, "Generation 9-11," *Newsweek,* November 12, 2001, pp. 53–54.

110. Quoted in Lynette Clemetson, "Kids Now Eager to Serve," *Newsweek,* November 12, 2001, p. 101.

111. Quoted in Donna Foote, "Islam, Arabic, and Afghanistan 101," *Newsweek,* November 12, 2001, p. 54.

112. Quoted in Kantrowitz and Naughton, "Generation 9-11," p. 48.

113. Adam, interview by author, Minneapolis, MN, October 1, 2001.

114. Gibbs, "If You Want to Humble an Empire," n.p.

For Further Reading

Ann G. Gaines, *Terrorism*. Philadelphia: Chelsea House, 1999. Well written, with good historical background on the use of terror. Excellent chapter on ways to combat terrorism.

Kathlyn Gay, *Silent Death*. Brookfield, CT: Twenty-first Century Books, 2001. A very inclusive look at chemical and biological weapons, and how they might be used by terrorist groups.

Laurel Holliday, ed., *Why Do They Hate Me?* New York: Pocket Books, 1999. Moving first-person accounts by children of the world who are living with wars and terrorism. Particularly good entries by Northern Irish, Palestinian, and Israeli children.

Pat Milton, *In the Blink of an Eye: The FBI Investigation of TWA Flight 800*. New York: Random House, 1999. Challenging reading, but excellent background on air safety and security issues.

Jim Ross and Paul Myers, eds., *We Will Never Forget: Eyewitness Accounts of the Bombing of the Oklahoma City Federal Building*. Austin, TX: Eakin Press, 1996. Helpful in understanding what had been, until September 11, 2001, the worst act of terrorism on American soil.

Victoria Sherrow, *The World Trade Center Bombing: Terror in the Towers*. Springfield, NJ: Enslow, 1998. Excellent photographs and helpful index.

Works Consulted

Jerry Adler, "Connecting in New York," *Newsweek Commemorative Issue: The Spirit of America,* n.d.

Jonathan Alter, "Patriotism: Filling the Demand," *Newsweek Commemorative Issue: The Spirit of America,* n.d.

Stephen Barr, "At the Pentagon, 'All of a Sudden . . . Anything But Routine,'" *Washington Post,* September 12, 2001.

Sharon Begley, "Protecting America: The Top 10 Priorities," *Newsweek,* November 5, 2001.

———, "The Rescue at the Pentagon," *Newsweek Commemorative Issue: The Spirit of America,* n.d.

———, "Will We Ever Be Safe Again?" *Newsweek,* September 24, 2001.

Lisa Beyer, "Is This What We Really Want?" *Time,* September 24, 2001.

———, "The Most Wanted Man in the World," *Time,* September 24, 2001.

"The Birds Are on Fire," *New York Times,* September 18, 2001.

Karen Breslau, "Courage in the Air," *Newsweek Commemorative Issue: The Spirit of America,* n.d.

Mark Clayton, "Controllers' Tale of Flight 11," *Christian Science Monitor,* September 13, 2001.

Lynette Clemetson, "Kids Now Eager to Serve" *Newsweek,* November 12, 2001.

John Cloud, "The Plot Comes into Focus," *Time,* October 1, 2001.

"Comment: Tuesday, and After," *New Yorker,* September 24, 2001.

"Crisis Management," *People Weekly,* September 24, 2001.

Anne Cronin, "A Black Cloud. A Shower of Glass. A Glimpse of Hell. Run!" *New York Times,* September 16, 2001.

Maureen Dowd, "A Grave Silence," *New York Times,* September 12, 2001.

Tom Downey, "LIVES; A Voice From the Rubble," *New York Times Magazine,* September 23, 2001.

Pat Doyle, "Under Suspicion: On Terror's Trail in Minnesota," *Star Tribune,* October 7, 2001.

Daniel Eisenberg, "Feeling the Heat from All Sides," *Newsweek Commemorative Issue: The Spirit of America,* n.d.

———, "How Safe Can We Get?" *Time,* September 24, 2001.

———, "Wartime Recession?" *Time,* October 1, 2001.

Marc Fisher and Don Phillips, "On Flight 77: 'Our Plane Is Being Hijacked,'" *Washington Post,* September 12, 2001.

Donna Foote, "Islam, Arabic, and Afghanistan 101," *Newsweek,* November 12, 2001.

David France, "Now, 'WTC Syndrome,'" *Newsweek,* November 5, 2001.

"From Our Correspondents," *New Yorker,* September 24, 2001.

Nancy Gibbs, "If You Want to Humble an Empire," *Time* (special edition), n.d.

———, "Life on the Homefront," *Time,* October 1, 2001.

———, "Shadow of Fear," *Time,* October 22, 2001.

Adam Gopnik, "The City and the Pillars," *New Yorker,* September 24, 2001.

"Hell on Earth," *People Weekly,* September 24, 2001.

"Helping Hands," *Newsweek Commemorative Issue: The Spirit of America,* n.d.

Michael Hirsch, "We've Hit the Targets," *Newsweek* (extra edition), n.d.

"I Saw Things No One Should Ever See," *Newsweek* (extra edition), n.d.

Richard Lenzin Jones, "A Growing Realization of Unspeakable Loss," *New York Times,* September 15, 2001.

Barbara Kantrowitz and Keith Naughton, "Generation 9-11," *Newsweek,* November 12, 2001.

Jeffrey Kluger, "Attack on the Spirit," *Time,* September 24, 2001.

Charles Krauthammer, "The Greater the Evil, the More it Disarms," *Time,* September 24, 2001.

Michael Lemonick, "The Next Threat?" *Time,* October 1, 2001.

"Lending a Hand," *People Weekly,* October 1, 2001.

John Michael Loh and Gerald Kauver, "FAA: A Failure on Aviation Security," *Aviation Week & Space Technology,* October 8, 2001.

Jim Lynch, ed., *The Day That Changed America* (American Media Publications special edition), n.d.

Johanna McGeary and David Van Biema, "The New Breed of Terrorist," *Time,* September 24, 2001.

Matthew Miller, "He's of Two Minds About Scrutinizing Arabs in Our Midst," *Star Tribune,* October 4, 2001.

"The Nation's Neighborhood," *Newsweek Commemorative Issue: The Spirit of America,* n.d.

"9.23.01: The Way We Live Now," *New York Times Magazine,* September 23, 2001.

James Poniewozik, "What's Entertainment Now?" *Time,* October 1, 2001.

Alexa Pozniak, "The Air We Breathe," ABC News.com, September 27, 2001. abcnews. go.com/sections/living/DailyNews/ WTC-gasmasks010926.html.

Amanda Ripley, "The Last Phone Call," *Time,* September 24, 2001.

Catherine Saint Louis, "The Looks They Get," *New York Times Magazine,* September 23, 2001.

Terence Samuel, "Plenty of Blame to Go Around," *U.S. News & World Report,* October 1, 2001.

"Saving Grace," *People Weekly,* September 24, 2001.

Roger Segelkin, "CU Veterinarian Aids Rescue Dogs at Site of World Trade Center," *Cornell Chronicle,* September 20, 2001. www.news.cornell.edu/Chronicles/9.20.0 1/WTC-dogs.html.

Jennifer Senior, "The Circles of Loss," *New York Magazine,* October 1, 2001.

Mary Beth Sheridan, "Loud Boom—Then Flames in Hallway," *Washington Post,* September 12, 2001.

Roger Simon, "A Test of Will," *U.S. News & World Report,* October 1, 2001.

Joel Stein, "Digging Out," *Time,* September 24, 2001.

Evan Thomas, "A New Day of Infamy," *Newsweek* (extra edition).

Evan Thomas and Mark Hosenball, "Bush: 'We're at War,'" *Newsweek,* September 24, 2001.

"A Tough Fight," *Time,* October 1, 2001.

Josh Tyrangiel, "Facing the End," *Time,* September 24, 2001.

"United States: Testing Intelligence, National Security," *Economist,* October 6, 2001.

David Van Biema, "As American As . . . ," *Time,* October 1, 2001.

———, "One God and One Nation," *Time,* September 24, 2001.

Dan Verton, "Security Experts Say Antiterror Information Tools Flawed," *Computerworld*, September 24, 2001.

Jodi Wilgoren and Edward Wong, "On Doomed Flight, Passengers Vow to Perish Fighting," *New York Times*, September 13, 2001.

Fareed Zakaria, "The End of the End of History," *Newsweek*, September 24, 2001.

Ricardo-Alonso Zaldivar, "After the Attack, Fateful Delay," *Los Angeles Times*, September 20, 2001.

Index

Picture Credits

About the Author

Gail B. Stewart received her undergraduate degree from Gustavus Adolphus College in St. Peter, Minnesota. She did her graduate work in English, linguistics, and curriculum study at the College of St. Thomas and the University of Minnesota. She taught English and reading for more than ten years.

She has written over ninety books for young people, including a series for Lucent Books called The Other America. She has written many books on historical topics such as World War I and the Warsaw ghetto.

Stewart and her husband live in Minneapolis with their three sons, Ted, Elliot, and Flynn; two dogs; and a cat. When she is not writing she enjoys reading, walking, and watching her sons play soccer.